**Issue 3** September 2000

**Edited by Dr. Valerie Steele**

# Fashion Theory

The Journal of Dress, Body & Culture

BERG

## Fashion Theory: The Journal of Dress, Body & Culture

### Editor

Dr. Valerie Steele
The Museum at the Fashion Institute of Technology, E201
Seventh Avenue at 27th Street
New York, NY 10001-5992
USA
Fax: +1 212 924 3958
e-mail: steelemajor@earthlink.net

### Book Reviews Editor

Christopher Breward
The London College of Fashion
20 John Princes Street
London W1M 0BJ

Please send all books for review to the Book Reviews Editor.

### Aims and Scope

The importance of studying the body as a site for the deployment of discourses is well-established in a number of disciplines. By contrast, the study of fashion has, until recently, suffered from a lack of critical analysis. Increasingly, however, scholars have recognized the cultural significance of self-fashioning, including not only clothing but also such body alterations as tattooing and piercing. *Fashion Theory* takes as its starting point a definition of 'fashion' as the cultural construction of the embodied identity. It aims to provide an interdisciplinary forum for the rigorous analysis of cultural phenomena ranging from footbinding to fashion advertising.

Anyone wishing to submit an article, interview, or a book, film or exhibition review for possible publication in this journal should contact Valerie Steele (at the address listed to the left) or the Editorial Department at Berg (150 Cowley Road, Oxford, OX4 1JJ, UK; e-mail: enquiry@berg.demon.co.uk).

Notes for Contributors can be found at the back of the journal.

ISSN: 1362-704X

| Ordering Information | Four issues per volume. | One volume per annum. | 2000: Volume 4 |
| --- | --- | --- | --- |

**By mail:** Berg Publishers, 150 Cowley Road, Oxford, OX4 1JJ, UK.

**By fax:** +44 (0) 1865 791165

**By telephone:** +44 (0) 1865 245104

**By e-mail:** enquiry@berg.demon.co.uk

**Inquiries** Editorial: Kathryn Earle, Managing Editor, e-mail: kearle@berg1.demon.co.uk

Production: Sara Everett. e-mail: severett@berg.demon.co.uk

Advertising + subscriptions: enquiry@berg.demon.co.uk

**Subscription Rates:** Institutional base list subscription price: £86.00, US$140.00. Individuals' subscription price: £35.00. US$55.00.

**Reprints of Individual Articles** Copies of individual articles may be obtained from the Publishers at the appropriate fees. Write to: Berg, 150 Cowley Road. Oxford. OX4 1JJ. UK.

Printed in the United Kingdom. SEPTEMBER 2000

Indexed by the International Bibliography of Social Sciences: The MLA International Bibliography; ARTbibliographies and Clothing and Textile Arts Index

Page 275

Page 245

Page 349

# Contents

**Editor**
**Dr. Valerie Steele**
The Museum at the Fashion
  Institute of Technology, E201
Seventh Avenue at 27th Street
New York, NY 10001-5992
USA

Fax +1 212 924 3958
e-mail: steelemajor@earthlink.net

BERG

*Fashion Theory*, Volume 4, Issue 3, pp.243–244
Reprints available directly from the Publishers.
Photocopying permitted by licence only.
© 2000 Berg. Printed in the United Kingdom.

© Roxanne Lowit

# Letter from the Editor

Yinka Shonibare is an extraordinary artist, and I am delighted to publish Janice M. Cheddie's analysis of his recent work, which draws attention to the way clothing constructs gendered and racialized identities. Shonibare creates facsimiles of the attire of Victorian bourgeois women, using a type of wax-printed cloth popularly associated in the west with traditional African dress, but which was actually produced by Dutch and English textile manufacturers as a commodity for the West African market. Both the production techniques and the designs on the cloth derive from their origin in Indonesia, then a Dutch colony. Thus, far from being the product of an African cultural identity, the cloth exposes a complex history of colonialism, trade relations, technologies of production and fashion. When this cloth is fashioned into garments for western "ladies," it opens up another discourse about femininity "within the signifying system of colonial relationships and power."

The subject of fashion in Africa is approached from another angle in Karen Tranberg Hansen's "Other People's Clothes? The International Second-hand Clothing Trade and Dress Practices in Zambia," which draws on her forthcoming book, *Salaula*. More than an analysis of the second-hand clothing trade, this is a cultural story about consumption and the way clothing can become an agent of social change. Hansen is especially insightful on the "influences from across the African continent

... that are establishing what is beginning to look like a pan-African fashion system." Her interviews also reveal the ways that gender influences the dress code.

Of course, this issue also includes several outstanding essays that are not on African fashion, on subjects as diverse as the dress of tourists in Nepal (Sharon Hepburn's "Cloth of Barbaric Pagans") and what might be called the body-clothes unit. In the latter, Anne Boultwood, a psychologist, and Bob Jerrard, Professor of Design Studies, analyze the subject of "Ambivalence, and Its Relation to Fashion and the Body," drawing on the sociological work of Susan Kaiser and the late Fred Davis, among others. In the course of her essay on the dressed body as situated practice, Joanne Entwistle provides a lucid summary of how the work of theorists such as Foucault and Bourdieu provides a useful framework for analyzing the discursive aspects of dress.

Four years ago I was putting together the first issue of *Fashion Theory*. Since then the journal has published dozens of articles and reviews by scholars and writers from a wide variety of disciplines. I had occasion to reread many of them this spring while teaching a course on "Visual Culture and Modern Fashion" at Columbia University. Although the students occasionally complained about the "pretentious" language in some of the articles, on the whole they seemed pleased to grapple with an intelligent discourse on fashion. Theorists like Michel Foucault, Judith Butler and Walter Benjamin did not faze them, although Jacques Lacan and Jacques Derrida proved more difficult to understand. At least they made an effort, which is more than can be said for some older scholars in the field of "costume studies."

Sometimes it seems ironic that I am editing a theoretical journal, since I myself was trained in the very down-to-earth, empirical discipline of history. Recently, some of the *Fashion Theory* gang were at an international conference on "The Discipline of Fashion," held in Dubrovnik, with participants from Britain, Croatia, France, Germany, Italy, Hungary and the USA. Barbara Vinken observed that there was a significant difference between the Anglo-American scholars, who were largely empirical in their approach, and the Europeans, who were much more likely to be students of semiotics and psychoanalysis. Since the middle is historically a dangerous position to occupy, I can only hope that I don't end up as the Kerensky or Danton of fashion theory... Meanwhile, I am organizing an exhibition on Leather at The Museum at the Fashion Institute of Technology, which will run from January through April 2001. If you are in New York then, please come to see it.

Sincerely yours,

Valerie Steele

*Fashion Theory*, Volume 4, Issue 3, pp.245–274
Reprints available directly from the Publishers.
Photocopying permitted by licence only.
© 2000 Berg. Printed in the United Kingdom.

# Other People's Clothes? The International Second-hand Clothing Trade and Dress Practices in Zambia

**Karen Tranberg Hansen**

Karen Tranberg Hansen is
Professor of Anthropology at
Northwestern University. She
has conducted research in
Zambia on urbanization, colonial
culture, work, and consumption
and is the author of several
books and articles on these
topics. She has just completed
her book on second-hand
clothing, *Salaula: The World of
Secondhand Clothing and
Zambia*, University of Chicago
Press, 2000.

World-wide exports of second-hand clothing from North America and
Europe have expanded rapidly in recent years, with spectacular import
increases in sub-Saharan Africa over the last two decades. Such clothing
is given many names in the countries that import it. It was called *Vietnam*
in Kivu in the eastern part of the former Zaire in the 1970s, and *calam-
idades* in Mozambique in the 1990s. It is known by local terms that mean
"dead white men's clothes" in Ghana, "died in Europe" in northwestern
Tanzania (Weiss 1996:138), and "shake and sell" in Senegal (Heath 1992:
28).[1] In East Africa it is called *mitumba*, which is Swahili for "bale." In
Malawi, it is *kaunjika*, which in Nyanja/Chewa means "to pick," while
in Zambia *salaula* means in Bemba "selecting from a pile in the manner
of rummaging."

The significance of these references to the West's clothing surplus depends on the case at hand and the economic and cultural politics of its time. What matters in Zambia is the way *salaula* names how people deal with clothing, selecting, and choosing garments to suit both their clothing needs and desires. Their concern with cutting a fine figure struck anthropologists in the past (Mitchell 1956; Richards 1969 [1939]; Wilson 1941–42) and their active preoccupations with clothing, style, and fashion continue to do so today. Because of the many influences on which clothing practices draw, Zambian dealings with clothing—both new and used, for of course they implicate one another—offer a particularly rich case for exploring some of the complex interactions between the local dress scene and its insertion in a variety of larger contexts.

Clothing, style, and fashion are important topics of everyday conversation in Zambia. The dressed bodies of persons of importance are the subjects of intense scrutiny and comment, as is the appearance of casual bystanders. Above all else, dress sensibilities in Zambia are visual and sensual. Created in performance, the aesthetic effect of the dressed body is a particular *look* that people strive to produce. The clothing competence they bring to bear on this process is extensive. Poor and rich, women and men, adolescent and adult, they all want to look "outstanding," "unique," or "exclusive." The meanings of clothes do not inhere in the garments themselves, but are attributed to them in ongoing interaction. That is to say that how clothing is construed and how it matters has a lot to do with the context in which it is worn. Even then, because individual dress practice does not always conform to widespread norms, the body surface easily becomes a battleground where questions about dress and its acceptability are tested.

On the pages that follow, I map out some of these processes in relation to Zambia, pointing to complex dialectics between the local clothing scene and its location in a larger context that includes other African countries, the West, Asia, and the mass media, among many other things. I begin with history, hinting at enduring entanglements between the second-hand clothing trade and current clothing consumption in the Zambian case. Then I sketch some contours of the international second-hand clothing trade and note some of its different dynamics across Africa. Next I turn to Zambia and the clothing consumption practices that have arisen around the rapidly growing import of second-hand clothing since the middle to late 1980s. I draw from research I have conducted since the early 1990s on the entire circuit of the international second-hand clothing trade from the point of sourcing in the West to the point where our used garments arrive in Zambia and enter into a local dress universe in which their meanings are redefined (Hansen 2000).

**Figure 1**
Sheltering from the sun under an umbrella. Young male second-hand clothing trader wearing untucked shirt on top of loose pants and "presidential shoes" (leather moccasins). Open-air section of Kamwala market, Lusaka. This section of the market was demolished in April 1999. Author's photograph, July 1992.

## The Second-hand Clothing Trade

In much of the West today, second-hand clothing makes up fringe, or
niche, markets. Income distribution, purchasing power, affordable mass-
produced garments and apparel, and concerns with fashion have reduced
the need for large segments of the population to purchase used clothing.
But well into the nineteenth century, used clothing constituted the effective
market for much of the population except the very rich. Still in many
countries in the Third World today, where the cost factor is enormously
important, second-hand clothing is both desired and needed. While
grinding poverty and deteriorating purchasing power as a result of
prolonged economic decline in most of the countries of sub-Saharan Africa
since the 1970s help explain why this region is the world's largest import
market for the lowest-quality used clothing, economics and poverty do
not adequately account for the popularity of a commodity like *salaula* in
Zambia. As I point out briefly below, the history of the second-hand
clothing system of provision feeds into and sharpens popular sensibilities
of clothing consumption.[2]

Past and present, the export trade in used clothing has been closely
linked to the costs of domestic garment manufacture in a process on which
historians have begun to throw light (Lemire 1997; Perrot 1994; Roche
1996). A detailed historical tracing of this trade is difficult because of
the very nature of second-hand clothing consumption, which tends to
exhaust the material evidence of its own past through extensive wear.
Until well after the beginning of ready-made garment production, clothes
went through many lives, passed down, resold or exchanged for other
goods, altered or mended, and resewn before they reached the final phase
of their journey and were recycled as rags into paper. "The success of the
second-hand clothes trade can only be commemorated," suggests the
costume historian Madeleine Ginsburg, "by their absence from museum
collections of material survivals. [But it] would be an injustice to pay a
similar complement to its history, of interest in its own right and as an
aspect of the garment history" (1980: 121).

By 1600, if not earlier, the second-hand clothing trade flourished in
major European cities, concentrated in specifically located markets, stores,
and pawnshops. The abandonment of guild regulations and sartorial dress
rules increased the demand for fashionable clothing, much of which was
satisfied from the second-hand clothing market (Lemire 1991a). Itinerant
"old clothes men" traded across the countryside in a process through
which garments continued to change hands (Lemire 1997: 75–93). From
the mid-eighteenth century on, the availability of more affordable cotton
and wool fabrics began gradually reducing home markets in second-hand
clothing at the same time as early mass producing tailoring firms made
new clothing more affordable (Lemire 1991b).

Like any other commodity in demand, second-hand clothing was
sourced and traded across vast distances. By the first half of the eighteenth

century, the Netherlands and London were centers for the wholesale trade in used clothes, with exports to Belgium, France, and South America. The export trade reached the colonies as well, including North America and Africa. By the late nineteenth century in Paris, reasonably priced ready-wear competed so effectively with second-hand clothes that the used clothing trade became limited to exports, especially to colonial Africa (Perrot 1994: 71).

The profitable potential of the second-hand clothes market in colonial Africa was seized after the two World Wars, when surplus army clothing was exported by used clothing dealers in America and Britain and on the Continent. The availability of army clothing and men's work clothing from the early production of ready-wear are among the reasons why the histories of second-hand clothing consumption in Africa are distinctly gendered. Men's greatcoats and jackets came first, and only in the inter-war period did women's wear begin to enter used clothing consignments for export. But the substantive growth of the African second-hand clothing export market is a phenomenon postdating the Second World War, a product both of supply and demand: a vast surplus of still wearable used clothing in the West, and growing desires and needs for clothes in Africa, where socioeconomic transformations catapulted more and more Africans into new markets as consumers.

## The Charitable Connection

Developments in the export trade in second-hand clothing since the Second World War have depended to a great extent on the clothing collection activities of major charitable organizations who supply both domestic and foreign second-hand clothing markets. The charities have a long, and changing, involvement with second-hand clothing. In both Europe and the United States at the end of the nineteenth century, philanthropic groups collected and donated clothes to the poor (Ginsburg 1980: 128). In the period after the Second World War, shifts in income distribution and growing purchasing power enabled more consumers than ever before to buy not only new, but more, clothes, including fashions and styles oriented toward specific niches, for example, teenage clothing, corporate and career dressing, and sports and leisure wear. Such dress practices produced an enormous yield of used, but still wearable clothes, some of which ended up as donations to charity.

Many charitable organizations began emphasizing store sales in the late 1950s, among them the Salvation Army, for which the sale of used clothing was the largest single source of income in the United States by the 1960s (McKinley 1986). The charitable organizations dominated the second-hand clothing retail scene in the 1960s and 1970s. During the 1980s, they were joined by a variety of specialist second-hand clothing stores that began to appear operating on a for-profit basis, with names, in the Chicago area, like Crowded Closet, Flashy Trash, Hollywood Mirror, Hubba Hubba, Bewitched, and Strange Cargo. Although most of the specialty resale stores cater to women, some stock garments for both sexes, and there are stores for children's clothing as well. Men's stores are beginning to appear—for example, Gentlemen's Agreement on the Upper East Side of Manhattan (*New York Times*, 14 December 1997, p. B14) and Second Time Around, in the middle of Boston's Newbery Street (*Wall Street Journal*, 20 January 1997, p. 1 and p. 6). Some stores operate on a consignment basis, selling "gently worn" designer clothes both for women and men; others source in bulk from commercial second-hand clothing vendors, or both.

Rarely featuring words like "used," "second-hand" or "thrift" in their names, most of these recent stores target specific consumers, for example, young professionals who may want high-quality clothes at modest prices or young people keen on retro and vintage fashion, punk, and rave styles (McRobbie 1989). There is a vigorous resale market for designer clothes in specialty stores whose customers buy designer labels to wear as "investment dressing," much as collectors buy art (*New York Times*, 4 June 1996, p. B11). And "thrift shopping" appears to have developed a new allure, providing pastime activity for vintage connoisseurs who are on the lookout for rare finds (*New York Times*, 28 September 1997, Travel section p. 27). Some of these businesses donate garments that do not sell well "to charity," and some also dispose of their surplus at bulk prices to commercial second-hand clothing dealers.

The charitable organizations are the largest single source of the garments that fuel today's international trade in second-hand clothing. Because consumers in the West today donate much more clothing than the charitable organizations can possibly sell in their thrift shops, the charitable organizations resell their massive overstock at bulk prices to commercial second-hand clothing dealers. While the spectacular increase in second-hand clothing exports to Africa since the mid-1980s has taken place alongside the growth of the international humanitarian aid industry, this export is less about charity than it is about profits. In fact, used clothing as outright donations in crisis and relief situations plays a very minor role in an export process that is overwhelmingly commercial.[3]

The second-hand clothing trade is an unusual industry with peculiar problems that arise from the uneasy relationship between "charity" and commercial interests and the ways that each of these is organized. In the West today, the second-hand clothing trade both in domestic and foreign markets is dominated by non-profit charitable organizations and private textile recycling/grading firms, often family-owned. Its financial side has largely eluded public scrutiny. Thriving by an ethic of giving in the West, the major charitable organizations look like patrons in a world-wide clothing donation project. Yet the major charitable organizations routinely sell a large proportion of their donated clothing, between 40 and 75 per cent depending on whom you talk to, to textile recyclers. Their extensive interactions with textile recyclers/graders add a commercial angle to their dealings about which there is little substantive knowledge. What is more, growing environmental concerns in the West in recent years have enhanced both the profitability and respectability of the rag trade and given its practitioners a new cachet as textile salvagers and waste recyclers.

From across the United States and northwestern Europe the textile recyclers/graders truck the used clothing they purchase in bulk from the charitable organizations to warehouses/sorting plants near major port cities. "Used clothing" includes not only garments but also shoes, handbags, towels, sheets, blankets, and draperies. The clothes are sorted by garment type, fabric, and quality before being compressed into bales. The standard weight is 50 kilograms; yet some firms also compress bales of much larger weights, usually of unsorted clothing. The clothes are often sorted under poor work conditions by poorly paid workers, some of whom are recent immigrants from countries where the clothes will be sold. The bottom quality goes to Africa, and medium quality to Latin America, while Japan receives a large portion of top-quality items, among which brand-name denim jeans and sneakers are in popular demand.

This sketch of some of the shifting contours of the second-hand clothing trade appears to explain its dynamics with reference to the history of clothing manufacture, first tailor-made and then factory-produced garments. But it is also, and in the longer haul, a cultural story about consumption and about the importance of clothing, both new and old, to modern sensibilities, embodying new social and cultural abilities to discriminate. In the process, clothing has become an important agent of social change (Martin 1994).

## World Exports and Imports

The second-hand clothing trade constitutes an immense, profitable, but barely examined world-wide commodity circuit that exports millions of dollars' worth of used clothing abroad. It grew more than sixfold over the last one and a half decades, from a value of US $207 million in 1980 to US $1,410 million in 1995 (UN 1996: 60).[4] The United States is the world's largest exporter in terms of both volume and value, followed by Germany, the Netherlands, Belgium-Luxembourg, and Japan. Between 1990 and 1995 alone, United States world-wide exports of this commodity doubled, from a value of US $174 million to US $340 million (UN 1996: 60).[5]

The countries of sub-Saharan Africa are the world's largest second-hand clothing destination, receiving in 1995 close to one-fourth of total world exports, worth US $379 million, up from US $117 million in 1990 (UN 1996: 60). There are several Asian countries among the large net importers of second-hand clothing, including Pakistan, Singapore, India, and Hong Kong. The large importers include such Middle Eastern countries as Syria and Jordan, as well as Malaysia and several countries in Latin America. Sizeable exports go not only to developing countries but also to Japan, the Netherlands, and Belgium-Luxembourg, which all engage in both import and re-export of this commodity.

African used-clothing markets undergo quick changes not only because of civil strife and war but also because of legislation guiding the entry or prohibition of second-hand clothing imports. Monetary policies affecting exchange rates and the very availability of foreign exchange influence the ability of local wholesalers to import. Some countries have at one time or the other banned imports, among them the Côte d'Ivoire, Nigeria, Kenya, and Malawi. Some countries have restrictive policies, for example South Africa, which only allows import of second-hand clothing for charitable purposes rather than for resale. Some small countries like Benin, Togo, and Rwanda before its civil wars, are large importers and active in transshipment and re-export. And although second-hand clothing imports are banned in some countries, there is a brisk transborder trade in this commodity.

## African Second-hand Clothing Markets

Second-hand clothing exporters need local knowledge not only about the political climate, import rules, tariffs, and currency regulations but also about clothing consumption practices in the various African countries. Some exporters have lived in Africa, and those who have not make on-site visits to familiarize themselves with local clothing markets. From the African end, wholesalers feed back information to their contacts in North America and Europe about which garments do and do not sell well.

Exporters need to reckon with considerable regional variation in Africa's clothing markets. In Muslim-dominated North Africa, for example, used clothing constituted only 7 per cent of total garment imports in 1980 compared to 33 per cent in sub-Saharan Africa (Haggblade 1990: 508–9). Tunisia is an exception to this with large imports, probably due to long practices of re-export (van Groen and Lozer 1976).

Local dress conventions differ in terms not only of religious norms but also of gender, age, class, and region, informing cultural norms of dress practice and influencing what types of garments people will wear and when. Briefly, in several countries in West Africa, distinct regional dress styles that are the products of long-standing textile crafts in weaving, dyeing, and printing today co-exist with styles of dressing introduced during the colonial period and after. In Nigeria and Senegal, for example, second-hand clothing has entered a specific niche. Although people from different socioeconomic groups, not only the very poor, now purchase imported second-hand clothing and use it widely for everyday wear, Senegalese and Nigerians commonly follow long-standing regional style

**Figure 2**
How many bras in a 50 kilogram bale? Sales display at Kamwala market, Lusaka. Author's photograph, May 1995.

conventions on important occasions, dressing with pride for purposes of displaying locally produced cloth in "African" styles (Denzer 1997: 10–12; Heath 1992: 21, 28). This is much in contrast to Zambia, where such textile crafts hardly existed and where people from across the socio-economic spectrum except at the very top are dressing in the West's used clothing. What is more, people in Zambia have been wearing Western-styled clothing since the early twentieth century, in fact for so long that they have made it their own. As a result, references to the West are not very helpful when explaining local dress conventions. Last but not least, there are invented dress "traditions." In Mobuto Sese Seko's Zaire, for example, the "authenticity" code forbade men from wearing Western coats and ties and women from wearing jeans. His successor, President Laurent Kabila of the Democratic Republic of the Congo, is conservative in matters of women's dress. One of his first edicts after assuming power in 1997 was to ban women's wearing of jeans and miniskirts (*The Post*, 22 July 1997, p. 10).

## The *Salaula* Market in Zambia

Zambia's second-hand clothing trade dates back to the colonial period, when imported used clothes reached Northern Rhodesia—as Zambia was called then—from across the border with the Belgian Congo, now the Democratic Republic of the Congo. Direct importation of this commodity was prohibited in Zambia during the first decades after independence in 1964. When restrictive import and foreign exchange regulations were relaxed in the middle to late 1980s, the second-hand clothing trade grew rapidly. The name *salaula* came into use at that time.

Figure 3
Wedding dress awaiting its
new bride. Next to it are
recycled sweatsuits, sewn
together by tailors from cut-up
pieces of unmatched
secondhand sweatshirts and
pants. Display inside Lusaka's
new City Market.
Author's photograph, August
1999.

**Figure 3**
Wedding dress awaiting its new bride. Next to it are recycled sweatsuits, sewn together by tailors from cut-up pieces of unmatched secondhand sweatshirts and pants. Display inside Lusaka's new City Market. Author's photograph, August 1999.

Second-hand clothing consignments destined for Zambia arrive by container ships in the ports of Dar es Salaam in Tanzania, Durban in South Africa, and Beira in Mozambique, from where they are trucked to whole-salers' warehouses in Lusaka, the capital. Lusaka is the hub of the *salaula* wholesale trade, though some firms have up-country branches. At the warehouse, marketeers, vendors, and private individuals purchase bales of *salaula*. They in turn distribute and sell their goods in urban and rural markets, hawk them in the countryside, and transfer them in rural exchanges in return for produce, goats, chicken, and fish. Today, in

**Figure 4**
Young male traders selling men's trousers and dress shirts. Ndola old Masala market.
Author's photograph, July 1993.

Zambia's urban and provincial markets, the *salaula* sections are many times larger than the food sections. *Salaula* is also sold from private homes in urban middle- and high-income residential areas, and some traders bring second-hand clothing to city offices and institutions like banks to sell on credit to employees who receive monthly paychecks.

The explosion of Zambia's *salaula* market has provided an income source for traders and created ancillary economic activities in repair, alteration, and support services for many others, including mature women and men, and a growing number of out-of-school youth, especially young men. In effect, in Zambia's declining economy, the *salaula* trade has created work opportunities for people who never held formal-sector jobs and for retrenched employees from both the public and private sectors. It also serves as a sideline for people who are seeking to extend their meagre earnings from jobs elsewhere. But above all, the *salaula* trade has made a profusion of clothing available from which dress-conscious consumers can purchase just the garments they want. "Watch Lusaka," suggested one writer. "All who are gorgeously attired mostly get their clothes abroad." Lusaka's so-called boutiques, he went on "have become rather like museums . . . neither Lusaka's Cairo Road nor the Kamwala shopping area is the place to look. You have a better chance at the second-hand clothes dealer, the flea market or even the city centre market dealer who jaunts between Lusaka and Johannesburg" (*Times of Zambia*, 26 August 1995, p. 4). He might have added what people in Zambia readily will tell you, namely that "three-fourths" of the population "shops from *salaula*." My survey observations about clothing consumption practices across class in Lusaka in fact confirm that popular impression.

## Zambian Clothing Profiles

What influences consumers in Zambia when they go about acquiring *salaula*? There is much more at stake in buying *salaula* than a mere exchange of cash, or barter, for clothes. Just as wholesalers of *salaula* are selective when ordering clothing consignments from the West to retail in local markets, so are consumers in their purchase of garments. Vital dimensions of the demand side are cultural taste and style matters. Indeed, consumption is hard work that may be understood through the practices and meanings consumers bring to bear on how they acquire and use things (de Certeau 1988:30–1).

When shopping from *salaula*, consumers' preoccupations with creating particular looks are inspired by fashion trends and popular dress cultures from across the world. Negotiating both clothing needs and desires, consumers are influenced by a variety of sources when they purchase garments. They draw on these influences in ways that are informed by local norms about bodies and dress. Above all, clothing consumption implicates cultural norms about gender and authority. Local notions of what to wear when and how to present the dressed body construct dress practice in Zambian terms that influence how people dress in garments from *salaula*. Clothing consumers speak of these terms in the language of tradition. Because this is a made up tradition, it is subject to change. That is why the normative terms for how to dress delineate rather than determine how people dress, leaving room for idiosyncratic and provocative dress practices as well.

To flesh out the normative aspects of Zambian dress practice I asked the persons I interviewed to describe both a well-dressed woman and a well-dressed man and to explain what made people look not well-dressed. These questions followed discussions of their favorite types of clothes and what they did not like to wear and why.[6] In fact, the two sets of questions complemented one another. The descriptions of well-dressed persons were remarkably uniform across the different residential areas in which I interviewed, constituting what amounts to a culturally dominant notion of how to dress—in effect, a dress code. Questions about hairstyles, make-up, and accessories supported these notions as well. Only in *apamwamba* (a Nyanja term, meaning literally "those on the top") households and women-headed households with ample economic means were these notions occasionally challenged. Some young adults also challenged, or wanted to challenge, these norms that circumscribed their clothing desires.

The composite clothing profiles of a well-dressed woman and a well-dressed man have much in common. The adult dress profile of both sexes is tidy, with smooth lines and careful color coordination. It is loosely fitting rather than tight. "Too many" different garments, colors, and fabrics distort the smooth profile, making the person look dishevelled, and drawing undue attention to the dressed body. Women's moderate use of jewelry and make-up, and the hairstyles of both sexes enhance the total

**Figure 5**
Formal suit profile. Young entry-level civil servant wearing his first suit, a double-breasted jacket with matching floral tie and handkerchief. Suit manufactured by local clothier, Serioes. Photographed by the author in Kabwe's *salaula* market, July 1993.

look to make it appear natural rather than artificial. In short, dress should complement the body structure and display it to its advantage.

For both sexes, these formal dress profiles convey notions about respectability and maturity, and of being in charge. Regardless of urban or rural residence, the accepted notion of how to dress makes adult men insist on suits, ties, long-sleeved shirts, and when of a certain age, hats for their public ensemble. Leather shoes, not boots, sneakers, or sandals, mark the man as properly put together. And irrespective of occupation and location, adult women insist on skirts below the knee, short-sleeved loose blouses or dresses, on top of which a *chitenge* (a wrapper of colorful printed cloth) can be worn if necessary and, when of a certain age, head-scarves; shoes with heels, not sandals, and certainly not sneakers, are part of their ensemble in public. But on the matter of how to present the dressed body the clothing profiles of women and men differ significantly. Women must cover their "private parts," which in this region of Africa includes their thighs. This means that dress length, tightness, and fabric transparency become issues in interactions with men and elders both at home and in public.

The active concern with cutting a good figure on Zambian terms is evident in the hard work of *salaula* consumption. That work includes shopping in the market, where consumers gather information on the availability of specific garments/styles and screen and sort products while they skillfully work their way through the piles of *salaula*, checking both for quality and style. They turn garments inside out to examine if the sewing is neat and whether there are rips or other flaws in the fabric. But the work of consumption extends far beyond the market. A well-dressed person is well-kempt herself, and her clothing is well kept. Producing the smooth, tidy clothing profile involves processes that easily escape the gaze of the casual observer or traveler, who sees *salaula* only as the West's cast-offs. The desire to be well turned out, even if the garments are second-hand, makes clothes-conscious Zambians insist on immaculate ensembles whose elements are carefully laundered and ironed. For this reason, the faded and torn jeans that are part of *salaula* bales imported from the United States are particularly unpopular. The desire to look spick and span prompts careful scrutiny of fabric quality to ascertain that colors of printed fabrics will not run in washing. Fading in sunlight is an issue as well. Most households do their laundry in cold water using strong detergents containing bleach, and clothes are usually hung up in the sunlight to dry. This is why color fastness and fabric quality are important issues in identifying clothes that are durable and will keep their good looks. And everyone pays great attention to shoes, commonly carrying a piece of cloth under the waist of a *chitenge* wrapper in their handbags or their pockets to remove Lusaka's dust when entering public buildings and private homes.

The attraction of *salaula* to clothing-conscious Zambian consumers goes far beyond the price factor and the good quality for money that many

**Figure 6**

Dress profiles. Women dressed for a public event, the annual Commercial and Agricultural Show in Lusaka. Styles from left to right: loose, short-sleeved blouse on top of straight skirt reaching below the knee, with a wrapper of printed cloth across the shoulder to carry a child; long-sleeved floral shirt on top of knee-length striped skirt; *chitenge* dress with matching wrapper and headscarf; and two-piece matching outfit of long-sleeved top in printed fabric and tiered skirt with paper cap carrying show design.
Author's photograph, July 1992.

of these garments offer. Above all, *salaula* makes available an abundance and variety of clothes that allow consumers to make their individual mark on the culturally accepted clothing profile. But the fact that we can identify Zambian terms for acceptable dress does not mean that everyone dresses alike. Nor does the desire to dress in "the latest" produce passive imitation and homogeneity. It is precisely the opposite effect consumers seek to achieve from *salaula* and that they find missing from much store-bought clothing: uniqueness. What they want are clothes that are fashionable rather than common. One of the women I interviewed in a high-income area put it this way when explaining why she shopped from *salaula*: "I don't want to wear what everyone else is wearing." "Clothes from *salaula* are not what other people wear," said another woman, explaining why they are viewed as "exclusive."

The desire for uniqueness, to stand out, while dressing the body on Zambian terms, produces considerable variations in dress in public workplaces and offices. Women never wear the same dress to work every day, according to their own reports, but rotate their garments and make new combinations of dresses and skirts. Their rotation occasionally includes dresses in a cut and style that in the West might be considered to be cocktail or evening wear. They may wear a *chitenge* dress to work as well, something rarely seen in the 1980s. In some banks and private firms, women wear suited uniforms, but have a "free dress" day once a week when they dress with their own sense of style.

Men work hard to achieve uniqueness in clothing presentation, too. Suits are worn in Zambia across a much wider range of the white-collar and civil service ranks than in the midwestern United States, for example. Civil servants rotate their immaculately kept suits, including older suits that wear the marks of time but always are crisply pressed. Young male bank tellers and clerical workers vary their suited look by wearing different types of shirt, tie and handkerchief combinations. Some men also wear jewelry, such as necklaces, tie-pins, bracelets, and rings, which they rotate. In fact men's suits are worn so commonly in Lusaka's downtown that, unlike in Harare, in neighboring Zimbabwe, you hardly ever encounter an adult Zambian man wearing shorts in public there.

Because notions of proper dress are context-dependent, their constraining effects may be temporarily put aside. This is the case on the urban disco and evening entertainment scene, which in the 1990s often displayed miniskirts and tight and transparent women's garments. Men who attend such events dress in designer jeans and trousers. And some could very occasionally be seen wearing the very high-waisted trousers inspired by Zairean rumba musicians. Specially styled jackets go with such trousers, adorned with a variety of inserted contrastive fabric or special collar, button, and pocket details. The majority of those who can afford to attend such events are of *apamwamba* background, the only group, as I suggested above, with an effective choice in the clothing market.

Last but not least, both play, idiosyncrasy, and pragmatics enter into how some people dress. I met many young men trading in the *salaula* markets who enjoyed dressing in a striking manner in garments they took a liking to. Examples include one young man who wore what looked like a hospital orderly's white uniform topped by a pink *peignoir*. Another young man dressed proudly in a church elder's purple gown. Dress practices such as these are not so much deliberate attempts to develop personal style distinctions as they are examples of the playfulness of young men who relish dressing up and showing off. This attitude of delight is

**Figure 8**
Scrutinizing *salaula* trousers. Man wearing tucked-in short-sleeved shirt, "twin cap" (two back pockets) trousers and leather shoes. Open-air section of Kamwala market, Lusaka. Author's photograph, July 1992.

also evident in the red nail polish that some young male street vendors paint on some, or all, of their fingers. "It looks good, we like it," they will tell you. What is more, the Zambian clothing scene is full of what to the Western eye may appear as unorthodox or incongruous styles, such as men wearing combinations of women's clothing, including coats, sweaters, and shorts, and women wearing men's dust coats and jackets. Such dress practices do not represent deliberate cross-dressing, but reflect the differential availability of women's and men's seasonal garments in the *salaula* consignments. Such clothing efforts are pragmatic aims at combining, for example, cold weather garments or work clothes from what is available from *salaula*.

## *Chitenge* Wear

The cultural constraints on Zambian women's dress practices are far more pronounced than those on men, who can create the smooth, continuous line enveloping their bodies to perfection from the combination of suit, shirt, and tie. Although Anne Hollander's work is inspired by clothing in Western art, some of her arguments resonate with widespread clothing sensibilities in Zambia. Her recent book emphasizes the enduring appeal of the suit in creating the "perfect man" (Hollander 1994: 92). She suggests that women's dress always makes a strong, almost theatrical, visual claim, while men's tailored suits set the real standard (1994: 8). Zambian women's commentaries on male and female clothing practice acknowledge such a difference almost in the same terms. Indeed, they complain that men have a much easier time dressing. In addition to being concerned with quality issues, color coordination, fit, and the right accessories, women have to worry about decency and respectability in dress. Yet there is one clothing platform where women take safe dress conventions in their own hands and develop them to the fullest. This is the two-piece *chitenge* outfit, the postcolonial creation of a women's national dress "tradition" that continues to take on new shapes, influenced in particular by Zairean and West African clothing trends. By contrast, West African-inspired loose gowns and print shirts have not appealed to Zambian men.

In the 1960s and 1970s, the *chitenge* suit consisted of a wrapper or plain skirt with a minimally tailored, short-sleeved, matching top and at times a headscarf. When the local textile factories still produced *chitenge*, their lines included not only colorful patterns but also commemorative designs, prints to promote for instance wildlife conservation or immunization, and announcements that made them into wearable political billboards (*New York Times*, 26 November 1989, section XX, p. 6 and p. 26). Women commonly then, as they still do today, wrapped lengths of *chitenge* cloth on top of a skirt or dress when working around the house or in the fields, traveling by public transportation, shopping in the public markets, or spending long waiting periods—for example on hospital

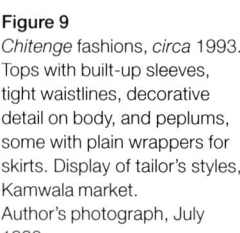

**Figure 9**
*Chitenge* fashions, *circa* 1993.
Tops with built-up sleeves,
tight waistlines, decorative
detail on body, and peplums,
some with plain wrappers for
skirts. Display of tailor's styles,
Kamwala market.
Author's photograph, July
1993.

grounds—and when attending overnight wakes and funerals. The most widespread use of *chitenge* is for carrying infants on the back. The *chitenge* holds bundles, serves as blanket when people sit on the ground, and has many other usages. As a constructed garment, the *chitenge* suit gradually became more elaborate during the 1980s. It has now evolved into a fashion that holds the ample breasts and hips that fit so uneasily into ready-made clothing and many of the dresses in *salaula* markets.

During the middle to late 1980s *chitenge* outfits were simple skirts or wraps and tops of printed fabric, at times with contrasting ribbons sewn around necks and sleeves; tie-dye became common then, often locally produced by West African women who taught Zambian women the technique; tie-dye was sewn up into loose garments, including trouser and top combinations, often with West African-styled embroidery around necks, sleeves, and edges. This may have been influenced by the feminization of the men's two-piece outfit of trousers and oversized tops that was popular in Nigeria in the late 1980s (Bastian 1996). The trouser and top profile changed during the first half of the 1990s to skirts and tops of printed cloth or tie-dye with marked waistlines, peplums, increasingly elaborate, built-up sleeves supported by interfacing, and with collars, necklines, and fronts embellished by contrasting material, buttons, ruffles, or smocking. There were several types of skirts to choose between: plain wrappers, double wrappers, and Tshala Muanas, pencil-tight skirts reaching below the knee with a long slit in front, named after a popular Zairean singer. In 1997, the latest style was inspired by West African dress and locally referred to as "Nigerian boubou."[7] This style consisted of huge flowing gowns of single-colored fabrics, damask or damask weave

**Figure 10**
Women dressed for kitchen
party in 1997.
From left to right: two-piece
suit, "office wear" of single-
colored top and floral skirt and
scarf; "Nigerian boubou" with
matching headdress; and two
versions of *chitenge* dresses
with built-up sleeves and a
variety of trim, with matching
headdress on the extreme
right.
Author's photograph, Lusaka,
August 1997.

imitations with elaborate embroideries in contrasting colors and with
accompanying built-up headgear. *Chitenge* fashions will no doubt continue to change, as their popularity rises or declines in interactions with
pan-African and global clothing trends. By 1999 in fact, the "boubou"
was not much in evidence. The preferred *chitenge* outfit that year featured
a straight skirt with a slit (worn in front or back) and a big sleeved blouse
with a variety of trimmings. Perhaps in Zambia, as has been suggested
for Kenya, this "global African dress signifies not tradition but modernity
... [that constructs] an elusive and ambiguous ... national identity"
(Rabine 1997: 163).

"You can do so many things with *chitenge*," explained one of the
teachers who kept account of her household budget and clothing expend-
itures for me. Her wardrobe consisted largely of *chitenge* outfits in some
of the different styles I just described and only a couple of "European-
styled" two-piece outfits. *Chitenges* are much more comfortable to wear,
she argued, than dresses and skirts "where you have to worry about belts
and matching blouses." Wearing *chitenge* is closely related to income, in
that the price of fabric and the tailor's charges might be too high for many
low-income consumers. A *chitenge* suit in 1995 easily cost K35,000 (more
than the average monthly wage of a domestic servant) when the price of
fabric, trimmings, and labor were added up and more, if the suit was
highly embellished. This is why the self-reported ratio of "European-
styled" to *chitenge* wear by low-income householders in my survey was
heavily skewed toward the "European" end, which in this case means
predominantly *salaula*. No one here claimed to wear only *chitenge*,
although some women had one or two outfits that they wore on special

occasions. In the high-income areas, by contrast, a small proportion of residents reported wearing only *chitenge*. Others wore *chitenge* with some regularity, and reported owning many suits. But "European-styled" clothing, which includes a high proportion of *salaula*, is the most widespread dress style here too.

Some women will tell you that they do not like *chitenge* outfits at all. Once pushed, they will explain that their dislike has to do with size, or "body structures" in the local dress language, meaning that they are "too" thin. Because of the body size factor, age plays into this preference as well, and young adult women do not in fact agree on whether or not they like *chitenge* fashions. "They do make big women look nice," said one young woman; whereas another complained that *chitenge* dresses only are for "old" women.

A good deal of clothing competence is entailed in purchasing attractive *chitenge* fabrics and identifying tailors who are able to deliver a finished product to the satisfaction of customers. Discriminating customers considered the *chitenge* fabric produced by the two formerly state-owned firms, Kafue Textiles of Zambia and Mulungushi Textiles until the early 1990s, to be of poor quality and unattractive design. Those who could afford it paid expensively on the black market for Dutch wax prints and *chitenges* brought across the border from Zaire and Burundi. The evaluation of *chitenge* depends not only on the attractiveness of the design but also on how well the fabric will keep after washing. Some *chitenges* contain a lot of starch and some have colors that run. In fact, *chitenge* dresses may not be very durable, which is one reason they have less appeal at the low-income level. Their short life is a product of mediocre fabric, frequent washing with strong detergents, and constant ironing,[8] often with a heavy charcoal iron, as many Zambian homes in the low-income areas are not electrified.

The increased availability in recent years of imported *chitenge* fabrics from India and Pakistan with attractive designs at more affordable prices and superior quality to those that used to be manufactured locally has helped to make *chitenge* fashions part of many more women's wardrobes than in the 1970s and 1980s. Office workers and teachers wear them to work, as do bank clerks on their "free dress" day. Above all, *chitenge* outfits are worn on formal visits and special occasions such as weddings and "kitchen parties" (bridal showers), where they are displayed proudly by mature women who have the body to carry them.

## Clothing, Gender, and Power

What Zambians describe as their dress "tradition" is not a static mold but an evolving set of practices in which different influences with various backgrounds are affecting one another, making it subject to variation over time as well as to resistance among some segments of consumers. Recent scholarship provides rich examples of the making and changing of "traditional" dress practices and their shifting cultural and political valuations (Ong 1990; MacLeod 1992). What is retained, borrowed or transformed in matters of dress depends a good deal on the cultural politics of its time. After Zambia's independence in 1964, the bush suit of colonial vintage with long trousers rather than shorts that the first president, Kenneth Kaunda, helped popularize as the safari suit came close to being considered men's traditional wear until the demise of the one-party state in 1991. The safari suit disappeared from the dress scene when the new president, Frederick Chiluba, chose to wear double-breasted suits with floral ties and matching handkerchiefs. Tailors got busy altering large-size single-breasted jackets into double-breasted jackets. Overnight, a new tradition of men's dress emerged, coinciding with the "new culture" associated with the opening up of both politics and economics.

Whether or not it has to do with politics, the general profile of the Zambian men's suited look has loosened up in the period during which I have paid close attention to dress practices. "Old people's styles are coming back," said one of the men I interviewed in 1997, no doubt thinking of the big trousers that were popular in the 1950s. The looser cut of men's suits today may in fact be influenced from the Zambian grass roots, by young male street vendors who since the early 1990s have been wearing looser and bigger clothes inspired by the American hip-hop and rap scene. Men used to insist on wearing shirts tucked in, well settled under their belts. Now not only street vendors wear their shirts loose, but also some white-collar workers. The loose shirt vogue has been legitimized by President Mandela, who, after taking office in South Africa in 1994, began wearing colorfully printed shirts, untucked, without

**Figure 11**
Male trader of second-hand suits, displaying and wearing a "new culture" suit himself. Inside section of Kamwala market, Lusaka. Author's photograph, May 1995.

jackets and ties, in public. "Mandela shirts" are often made of paisley-inspired print fabrics, and they are among the garments the suitcase traders bring back to Zambia from their shopping trips to South Africa.

Aside from the flourishing of *chitenge* fashions, less has changed in the realm of women's clothing, except perhaps for the sleeveless blouse and dress, which of late have become fairly widespread among younger consumers. But issues about women wearing short skirts and dresses, tight clothing, and trousers continue to agitate some segments of society. Young women's dressed bodies receive considerably more critical scrutiny than men's. This has been dramatized in Lusaka by intense reactions to repeated stripping incidents of young women wearing miniskirts in public throughout the 1990s. These sadly recurring events show that women's dress options in public settings where men are present are very circumscribed, and that challenge of what amounts to a dress code easily provokes men to verbal harassment and more. I have dealt with the miniskirt issue in some depth elsewhere (Hansen n.d.), and turn here to some examples of young men's dress practice.

If miniskirts, jeans, and dresses indexed young adult women's anxieties about their future possibilities and position in Zambia during the last half of the 1990s, so did suits and jeans for their young male age-mates, yet with different ramifications. Unlike young women, who carefully monitor the way they dress in public, young men like to draw attention to themselves, in different ways to be sure, depending on their socio-economic circumstances and regional location in Zambia's declining economy. For example, many young urban men close to secondary school graduation looked forward to wearing suits. Formal suits indexed their desire to lead adult, responsible, working lives, when as household heads they would become the men in charge. They were ambivalent about wearing jeans, which in their view too readily call forth the image of scruffy youths and street vendors, who are viewed in some circles as a threat to society's stability and security. Because I was curious about the evolving street vendor style scene and its influence on mainstream dress in Zambia, I explored it in more detail in 1997 through a brief survey of young men who stood out from the street crowd because of their dress and young entry-level civil servants, who were taken note of because of their sharp suits.[9]

The young street vendors were interviewed in public places where they work and relax, such as markets, streets, bus stops, and bars, while the young civil servants were interviewed in a basketball club. They ranged in age from 19 to 22; a few of them had completed grade 12, while the rest had dropped out of school earlier. The most striking observation, which complements my findings from interviewing *salaula* traders of this age-range in the markets, is that no one was married; most of them lived with their parents or guardians, intermittently helping out with household expenses; some of them lived in rented rooms they shared with friends who all were "in business," in one case the *salaula* trade in exchange for rural produce, and in another the suitcase trade to the south. They all preferred to dress in jeans styles. In addition to the style explanations I describe below, their preference for denim fabric has a clear practical reason. Jeans, one of them explained, "are durable; they are nice and easy to keep, especially by bachelors like me who have no one to look after our clothes."

What these young men did for their own pleasure was to dress up in public in variations on the baggy jeans look, several sizes larger than in 1995, and often wearing more than one set of clothes. The interviews did take place during the southern hemisphere's coldest months, when many people often wear garments on top of one another; yet the layered look was definitely in. In fact by 1999, the layered look had acquired a name of its own, *bombasa*, which had also inspired a new rap song (*Zambia Daily Mail*, 3 September 1997, p. 7). They did wear other styles. A couple of the young men wore oversize shorts, of the kind that hang down below the knee and were locally referred to as "hot pants." Unlike American rappers, whose brand name underwear is often visible underneath the layer of pants, these young men's underwear did not show. They all wore oversize tops, often with hoods. The preferred headgear had changed since 1995 from the baseball cap to knitted wool caps locally referred to as "headsocks," often with a pattern in multi-colored stripes, and occasionally a name or a logo. There were fewer hightop sneakers around than in 1995; the preferred footwear of the 1997 season was shoes with thick-treaded rubber soles leaving tractor-like imprints, called "galagata" (in Bemba, *ukukalakata* refers to walking with footwear that makes a noise). The young men often wore their shoes without socks. Several of them had an ear-ring in their left ear, one sported a nose-ring, and many wore bracelets.

These young men purchased their clothing from the "Zambia–Zaire" sections on the periphery of the city markets, where garments from "outside" were for sale; some used the tailor for special wear; and most of them scoured the *salaula* markets for just the right items. As one of them explained: "in *salaula* you will find things you can't believe how good they are." They readily pinpointed the inspiration of their style: friends from around town, local people that are admired, and foreigners. Foreign influences from a variety of sources enter through magazines, posters, music videos, television, and the cinema. Although a television set is far from being a common fixture in all households in Zambia's low- and medium-income residential areas, viewing it is often a shared experience that may include neighbors and friends. Many bars have TVs and VCRs. What is more, informal video parlors are appearing in the low-income areas where music videos draw an attentive audience, especially of young men. Clearly, young men such as these are exposed to multiple dress influences.

"I wear the big look because it is fashion," one of these young men said, while another explained that he liked to "move with time." "I don't like common clothes and imitations," said yet another. When shopping for clothes, these young men look for garments that will contribute to the overall creation of a particular style, in this case "the big look," rather than for brand-name items. Their dress style is far less glamorous than that of the *sapeurs* in Congo-Brazzaville, who, at least according to accounts prior to the recent civil war, celebrated appearance by parading expensive, upscale clothing they had obtained in Paris, proudly displaying *la griffe*, the label (Gandoulou 1989: 12–13). Like the women I described earlier, who wanted fashion and pieced their dress ensembles together from *salaula* to achieve what they considered to be uniqueness and exclusivity, these young street vendors strive for a particular look, and they also want fashion. And fashion does not mean homogeneity; while dressing almost alike, these young men in fact were hard at work on attaining "distinction," which is why they do not like "common clothes and imitations" but something that is "outstanding" and makes people look. "The big look," one of them said, "gives me confidence in myself."

The "big look" has been incorporated into the casual wear that young civil servants put on during weekends; and it has, as I noted earlier, affected the general suit profile. How young civil servants dress depends on the situation, and they have more choices than the street vendors. These young men, who ranged in age from 22 to 26, wore formal suits to work, and they liked them. They were all married with children, except for one who lived with his fiancée. Shopping from the same sources as the street vendors, they strive for the executive look, which they explained in terms fairly similar to those used by the street vendors. Clothes like these, one said, "make me look good and elegant and different from my age group. I don't like common clothes. Besides," he added, "ladies like nice clothes and I like to attract ladies." Two of these young civil servants spoke specifically about disliking "West African attire" with big, loose tops in bright colors and prints and simple pajama-like drawstring trousers underneath. Zairean-inspired high-waisted trousers of the kind often worn by rumba musicians were not popular at all with any of these young men.

The "big look" the young street vendors work so hard to achieve through what they consider to be just the right combinations of clothes sometimes comes with an attitude that is inflected in language use and an intonation that has given them the name "yoo boys." "They are performing," said an elderly man who was commenting on the big look, "they want to identify differently from ordinary people. They can take these clothes off again." But even if these young men take their clothes off again, their life chances are not likely to improve considerably. Their dress style is not part of a subculture in the sense described by Dick Hebdige that sneers at mainstream dress conventions (1988). Instead, they dress to escape their own economic powerlessness, momentarily and vicariously; and so they put on clothes they equate with power and success. The young male secondary school students who spoke disparagingly about the street vendors' get-up fear ending up like them. Will they themselves after completing secondary school face unemployment and perhaps dead-end jobs, like the street vendors, who earn too little to set up households of their own? It is not in the least surprising that many of them liked suits, which, on their horizon, given the economic situation in Zambia, index formal employment, wages, household comforts, and the power that comes from being men in charge.

## Other People's Clothes?

In everyday talk in Zambia, few would think of blaming the West for affecting clothing consumption whether new or old, and there is no suggestion of *salaula*'s being the flip side of Western fashion. In fact, people here rarely use the category "the West." Instead they talk about the "outside," which includes neighboring countries in the region, as well as Hong Kong and the United States. Or they invoke the "well developed countries" or "the donor countries." This is not surprising since, after all, in the postcolonial era, especially from the mid-1970s on, "development" has been the principal avenue through which "the West" has affected their lives. They also use terms that emerge in the context of specific encounters, for instance the United States, the United Kingdom or India. Their narratives employ changing idioms of time and place that are indicative of the varying types of exposure to the world beyond home among the generations who grew up prior to and after independence.

What the West is, above all, is an imagined place, associated with power, wealth, and an abundance of consumer goods that surpass most local products in quality and style. From it comes, for example, via American youth subculture, the hip-hop and rap-inspired style of young male street vendors in Zambia. Yet women's two-piece outfits are not American-derived, but influenced rather by British and South African fashions. Distinctions between Zambian styles and dress styles in America, Britain, South Africa, and elsewhere obscure dynamic relationships and influences that cross such boundaries, producing creative tensions that energize the everyday world of dress practice. There is a multiplicity of heritages at work here, with complex dialectics between local and foreign influences, and between what is considered to be "the latest" and what is current, in a reconfiguration process that generates distinct local clothing consumption practices.

The popularity of *salaula* as an element of dress practice in a developing country like Zambia offers interdisciplinary scholarship on dress and popular culture several important insights. First of all, dress conventions in Zambia are the outcomes of multiple interactions that engage style-conscious individuals with influences from many different parts of the world. Prominent in the dress practices I have described in this article are inspirations from across the African continent, particularly in women's dress, through processes that are establishing what is beginning to look like a pan-African fashion system in its own right. The second insight concerns matters of cultural taste and style that are embedded in a complex host of local social and cultural processes. These processes have worked themselves out differently across the generations, by class, and, as I have shown here, particularly by gender. This insight adds a startling twist to conventional assumptions about gender and dress that have tended to attribute late twentieth-century concerns with style and fashion to women. For in the case of Zambia, adolescent girls and adult women have far less scope for experimentation with clothing than men, for whom local society allows more room to move with fashion. And the last but not the least compelling insight arising from this study of second-hand clothing consumption is that being poor and being a discriminating consumer are not mutually exclusive.

## Acknowledgments

The original version of this paper was prepared for a theme presentation at the annual meeting of the International Textile and Apparel Association held at Santa Fe, 11–13 November 1999. I am enormously grateful to Mary Littrell for inviting me and to members and participants for their response. My revisions have benefited from the constructive input of Valerie Steele and members of her editorial board. The discussion draws on preliminary work I carried out in Zambia during the summers of 1992 and 1993, extensive field research and archival work conducted in Zambia, the southern African region, and Europe during the calendar year of 1995, continued work in Europe during the summer of 1996 and the spring and summer of 1997, and returns to Zambia during the summers of 1997 and 1999. The research has been supported by faculty grants from Northwestern University and awards from the Social Science Research Council (USA) and the Wenner Gren Foundation for Anthro-pological Research. Many of the points presented in this paper are developed in more depth in my book (Hansen 2000).

## Notes

1. I thank Jacques Depelchin, Roger Sanjek, Kathie Sheldon, and Teodosio Uate for these insights.
2. In my book (Hansen 2000) I use the notion of a system of provision (Fine and Leopold 1993) to analyze the entire economic circuit of the second-hand clothing trade, beginning with production in the form of sourcing, distribution and exchange, and consumption. I also explore the changing history of this system, paying particular attention to its developments since the Second World War.

3. In recent disaster situations, some relief organizations have urged the public to give money rather than foodstuffs and used clothing. According to the Red Cross, such donations can impede relief efforts because of the time and cost involved in collection, sorting, transportation, storage, and distribution (*Tampa Tribune*, 30 October 1998, p. 3).

4. These statistics must be interpreted with many qualifications. There is a widespread tendency to underreport both the value and volume of shipments for export in order to reduce shipping costs and import tariffs. The main statistical source, the United Nations international trade statistics, are not complete. Not all countries report to the United Nations, and even if they report, they might undervalue the extent of trade. And when they exist, many import statistics are misleading because of extensive smuggling.

5. According to a specialist from the US department of commerce, that amount represents only what is shipped abroad in compressed bales, and does not include garments piled loosely in containers as filler or smuggled across the Mexican border. He estimated the total export to be double the official figure (*Plain Dealer*, 25 January 1998, p. 6H).

6. My approach to these questions was influenced by Rick Wilk's (1997) constructive suggestion that exploring what people "hate to" consume casts critical light on desire and preference.

7. The term *boubou* is used in Francophone African countries for women's tunic-like dresses. The reference to "Nigerian boubou" in Zambia is an example of the extent of cross-over inter-African influences in dress styles.

8. Larvae from eggs laid by *putsi* flies on wet laundry easily enter the skin of a person, producing a boil-like swelling. To prevent this from happening, local and expatriate women alike insist that all clothing that has been dried in the open must be carefully ironed.

9. Oscar Hamangaba conducted this exercise for me in 1997. Aside from exploring the source of these young men's clothing, he engaged them in conversation about why they dressed in this manner. He asked questions about their personal circumstances as well.

## References

Bastian, Misty. 1996. "Female 'Alhajis' and Entrepreneurial Fashions: Flexible Identities in Southeastern Nigerian Clothing Practice." In Hildi Hendrikson (ed.), *Clothing and Difference: Embodied Identities in Colonial and Post-Colonial Africa*, 97–132. Durham, NC: Duke University Press.

de Certeau, Michel. 1988. *The Practice of Everyday Life*, trans. Steven Kendall. Berkeley, CA: University of California Press.

Denzer, LaRay. 1997. "The Garment Industry under SAP with a Special Case Study on Ibadan." Unpublished paper presented in workshop on

SAP and the Popular Economy. Development Policy Centre, Ibadan, Nigeria. August.

Fine, Ben and Ellen Leopold. 1993. *The World of Consumption*. London: Routledge.

Gandoulou, Justin-Daniel. 1989. *Dandies à Bacongo: Le culte de l'élégance dans la société congolaise contemporaine*. Paris: L'Harmattan.

Ginsburg, Madeleine. 1980. "Rags to Riches: The Second-Hand Clothes Trade 1700–1978." *Costume* 14: 121–35.

Haggblade, Steven. 1990. "The Flip Side of Fashion: Used Clothing Exports to the Third World." *Journal of Development Studies* 26(3): 505–21.

Hansen, Karen Tranberg. 2000. *Salaula: The World of Second-hand Clothing and Zambia*. Chicago: University of Chicago Press.

——. n.d. "Dressing Dangerously: Miniskirts, Gender Relations and Sexuality in Zambia." Unpublished manuscript under review.

Heath, Deborah. 1992. "Fashion, Anti-Fashion, and Heteroglossia in Urban Senegal." *American Ethnologist* 19(2): 19–33.

Hebdige, Dick. 1988. *Subculture: The Meaning of Style*. London: Routledge.

Hollander, Anne. 1994. *Sex and Suits: The Evolution of Modern Dress*. New York: Alfred A. Knopf.

Lemire, Beverly. 1991a. *Fashion's Favourite: The Cotton Trade and the Consumer in Britain, 1660–1800*. Oxford: Oxford University Press.

——. 1991b. The Nature of the Second-Hand Clothes Trade: The Role of Popular Fashion and Demand in England, *c*.1700–1850." In CISST (ed.), *Per una storia della moda pronta: problemi e ricerche* (Atti del V Convegno Internazionale del CISST Milano, 26–28 febbraio 1990), 107–16.

——. 1997. *Dress, Culture and Commerce: The English Clothing Trade before the Factory, 1660–1800*. New York: St Martin's Press.

McKinley, Edward H. 1986. *Somebody's Brother: A History of the Salvation Army's Men's Social Service Department 1891–1985*. Lewiston, NY: Edwin Mellen Press.

MacLeod, Arlene E. 1992. "Hegemonic Relations and Gender Resistance: The New Veiling as Accommodating Protest in Cairo." *Signs* 17(3): 533–57.

McRobbie, Angela. 1989. "Second-Hand Dresses and the Role of the Ragmarket." In Angela McRobbie (ed.), *Zoot-Suits and Second-Hand Dresses: An Anthology of Fashion and Music*, pp. 23–49. London: Macmillan.

Martin, Phyllis M. 1994. "Contesting Clothes in Colonial Brazzaville." *Journal of African History* 35(3): 401–26.

Mitchell, J. Clyde. 1956. *The Kalela Dance*. Rhodes-Livingstone Papers no. 27.

Ong, Aihwa. 1990. "State versus Islam: Malay Families, Women's Bodies, and the Body Politic in Malaysia." *American Ethnologist* 17(2): 258–76.

Perrot, Philippe. 1994 [1981]. *Fashioning the Bourgeoisie: A History of Clothing in the Nineteenth Century*, trans. Richard Bienvenu. Princeton, NJ: Princeton University Press.

Rabine, Leslie W. 1997. "Not a Mere Ornament: Tradition, Modernity, and Colonialism in Kenya and Western Clothing." *Fashion Theory* 1(2): 145–68.

Richards, Audrey I. 1969 [1939]. *Land, Labour and Diet in Northern Rhodesia*. Oxford: Oxford University Press.

Roche, Daniel. 1996 [1989]. *The Culture of Clothing: Dress and Fashion in the Ancien Regime*, trans. Jean Birrell. Cambridge: Cambridge University Press.

UN (United Nations). 1996. *1995 International Trade Statistics Yearbook 1994. Vol. II: Trade by Commodity*. New York: United Nations.

van Groen, Barth and Piet Lozer. 1976. *La Structure et l'organisation de la friperie à Tunis*. Groupe d'études Tunis. Amsterdam: Université Libre Amsterdam.

Weiss, Brad. 1996. "Dressing at Death: Clothing, Time, and Memory in Buhaya, Tanzania." In Hildi Hendrickson (ed.), *Clothing and Difference: Embodied Identities in Colonial and Post-Colonial Africa*, 133–54. Durham, NC: Duke University Press.

Wilk, Richard. 1997. "A Critique of Desire: Distaste and Dislike in Consumer Behavior." *Consumption, Markets, and Culture* 1(2): 175–96

Wilson, Godfrey. 1941–42. *An Essay on the Economics of Detribalization, Vols 1 and 2*. Rhodes-Livingstone Papers nos. 5 and 6.

**Newspapers**

*The Post* (Zambia). 1997. Caution Kabila (editorial). 22 July, p. 10.

*New York Times*. 1989. Zambia's Social Fabric. 26 November, section XX, p. 6 and p. 26.

— —. 1996. Glad Rags to Riches in the Resale Market. 4 June, p. B11.

— —. 1997. Secondhand Souvenirs. 28 September, Travel section p. 27.

— —. 1997. Big-Men's Wear, from a Stranger's Closet. 14 December, p. B14.

*Plain Dealer*. 1998. America's Old Clothes Finding Homes Abroad. 25 January, p. 6H.

*Tampa Tribune*. 1998. Red Cross Needs Cash to Help after Georges. 30 October, p. 3.

*Times of Zambia*. 1995. Wanted: Quality Clothing in Zambia (by Samuel Ngoma). 26 August, p. 4.

*Wall Street Journal*. 1997. Second-Hand Rows: These Thrift Shops are Classy—and Doing a Booming Business. 20 January, p. 1 and p. 6.

*Zambia Daily Mail*. 1999. "Nasty D" Makes Debut Performance. 3 September, p. 7.

*Fashion Theory*, Volume 4, Issue 3, pp.275–300
Reprints available directly from the Publishers.
Photocopying permitted by licence only.

# The Cloth of Barbaric Pagans: Tourism, Identity, and Modernity in Nepal

**Sharon Hepburn**

Sharon Hepburn lived in Nepal from 1990 to 1993, trying to understand how Nepali people make sense of the people, ideas, and things associated with modernity. Her 1997 Ph.D. from Cornell, based on this research, explores parallels between visual and social perception. At present she teaches Anthropology at Trent University in Canada.

In 1986 I was standing with a Nepali friend in Thamel, the tourist ghetto of Kathmandu. A tourist walked by wearing a style of hat that was then being sold in the shops around Thamel: the hat was flat-topped and rested high on the crown, and the front was made from brightly colored fabric (Figures 1 and 2). Kiran's family owns two hotels, and he has seen many tourists and is familiar with their ways. He watched the tourist and— understanding that the tourist believed he was wearing a local fashion— commented: "I have never seen a Nepali wear a hat like that." And neither, I concurred, had I. When I returned to Nepal in 1990,[1] however, things had changed: wearing the hats had become fashionable amongst some Nepalis, particularly young high-caste Hindu men, as well as with tourists and to some degree also in North America.

**Figure 1**
Thamelcloth hat and jacket
worn by a model in an
American catalog.

**Figure 2**
Variations on the Thamelcloth
hat (on the right-hand side,
and bottom left) from a Nepali
export catalog.

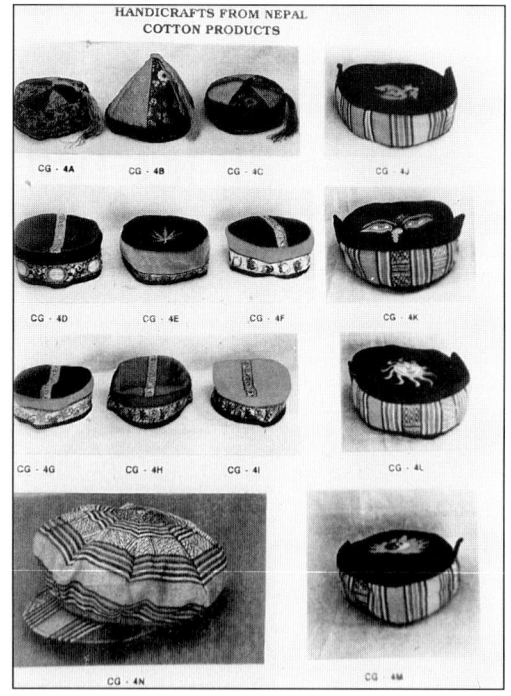

In this article we shall follow the cloth these hats are made from, through the markets and imaginations of people in Kathmandu, and across the Pacific to North America. We shall follow the cloth as it is materially produced, and as it is marketed as a representation of Tibetanness. And we shall follow it through its appropriation by some Nepali people, as a means to identify with the intended consumer, the tourist. Put simply, the fabric and clothes are made to appeal to tourists' conception of Nepaliness or Tibetanness, especially as that interfaces with ideas of human rights; some Nepalis, associating the clothing with tourists, then buy it because they associate it with the tourists, modernity, and "fashion."

These garments, then, are variously understood and used as expressions of identity, within different but overlapping social contexts, in times of change. These clothes also, like all clothes, are signs within particular systems. Yet, if there is a language of fashion (Calefato 1997), in this case it is spoken and read from multiple social and cultural locations, such that there is a "symbolic surplus" (Kristeva 1969, cited in Calefato 1997) from the shifting of signifiers. The various wearers and observers of these clothes originally made as tourist souvenirs live in worlds of meaning that are in some ways distinctly different, yet that nonetheless intersect through global processes of tourism, media, and political ideologies. The anthropologist Renato Rosaldo (1989) calls these places of intersection "borderzones," that is, areas between cultures that are places of cultural creativity. I propose that within these cultural borderzones, people appropriate sartorial items to identify where they stand in the ever-shifting social landscape. In this process, the cloth in question—hereafter called "Thamelcloth," after the low-budget tourist area of Kathmandu—is a multivalent sign facilitating creativity in the borderzones where cultural horizons intersect.

## The "Tourist" Caste in the Social Landscape of Nepal

To begin to explore the questions of identity that are played out and expressed around this clothing, we need to understand that "Tourist" is a racial/ethnic category (therefore and hereafter capitalized) in Nepal. We also need to understand how Tourists fit into the social horizons that Nepali people look out on, and in which they imagine and experience both themselves and their clothing choices. To begin, some examples would be useful.

I was once speaking with a man who has a store in Kathmandu offering items appealing to tourists, including the Thamelcloth clothing. "Who buys these things?" I asked; "Tourists . . ." he answered, ". . . and some Japanese." A man running a tourist hotel heard me addressed by my Nepali name (Chandra Maya) and asked what my "Tourist name" was: "Sharon" was my answer. I once asked a man when he had first met a tourist, and he replied: "Oh, about ten years ago, in my village, when UNICEF put in water pipes and the project director was a Tourist, a German."

From conversations such as these, and many others, it is clear that for many people in Nepal, a Tourist is not a person who puts aside more lasting identities in order to travel, as Smith (1978) and others suggest in terms of Western commonsensical categories. Rather, for Nepalis the word often brings to mind a kind of person—white, "developed"—and it is used as a racial/ethnic/cultural/caste designation within an idiom of personhood common throughout south Asia. Thamelcloth clothing is linked—to put it in the strongest form—to a caste group, the Tourist caste group. In a less strong form, it is fair to say that the clothing is linked to a group with very caste-like qualities, the Tourists. This is significant, because clothing in Nepal is strongly linked to caste/ethnic identification: clothing is a system of signs whose meaning rests within the syntagmatic frame that is the caste system. How the Thamelcloth clothing figures in the Nepali imagination, then, is rooted in the social and cultural foundations of the Nepali state, and in the notion of personhood they rest on.

**Figure 3**
Tourist Jeff wears a jacket with Thamelcloth variation trim. His shoulder bag has "classic" Thamelcloth pattern trim.

The Nepali state was created in 1769, founded by Prithvi Narayan Shah, who sought to organize his newly conquered and consolidated lands by creating a caste system in which to place the disparate people who inhabited the territory that was to be the new Nepal (Stiller 1973). He modeled the new social order on the fourfold classification of people common throughout South Asia, and describes Nepal as a "garden" with thirty-six species of "flower," or *jaat* organized into four *varna*s. The *varna*s are, in descending hierarchical order, the *Brahmin*s (priests), the *Kshatriya*s (warriors/rulers), the *Vaisya*s (merchants/artisans), and the *Sudra*s (servants). Even lower than these are the Untouchables—sometimes thought of as a fifth *varna*—who are people who do work judged within the Hindu world to be ritually polluting. This untouchable category includes butchers, sweepers, blacksmiths, and—most important in this discussion of clothing—tailors and seamstresses.

*Jaat* here means species, or type, or sort, and the word is often used interchangeably—by English-speaking Nepalis and foreigners alike—with the word "caste." Dumont tells us that the word "caste" comes from the Spanish and Portuguese "casta," which means "something not mixed" (1980: 21). Marriot and Inden (1985) tell us that the word has its origins in an Indo-European verbal root meaning "genesis," "origin," or "birth," and can be used to describe any kind of living thing, including, among humans, "a distinct sex, a race, a caste, or a tribe; a population, the followers of an occupation or a religion, or a nation" (Marriot and Inden 1985: 349). In Nepal all these usages are current: I have heard people speak of "the women's caste," "the American caste," as well as the various castes/ethnic groups defined by Prithvi Narayan Shah.

Thus, the new state of Nepal created a caste system based in the idea of kinds of people sharing an essential quality, separate from other kinds of people, and arranged hierarchically in terms of purity. The Brahmins and Chetris at the top were purest; the untouchables at the bottom were impure and did the ritually defiling work of society; and the Tibetans/ Bhotes (whether from north of the Nepali border, or descendants of a long history of migration south into Nepal) were ranked as "enslavable alcohol-drinkers" in the middle ranges of the caste hierarchy, above the untouchables, but considerably lower than the Brahmins and Chetris (Hofer 1979:45). The enterprise of making, selling, and consuming the Thamelcloth clothing is structured by the caste system. Among the actors in this article and in the business, the division of expressive and actual labor is as follows: Some high-caste Brahmins and Chetris (along with others) wear some of the Thamelcloth clothing, and the untouchable tailors (along with others) make the clothes. The Tibetans/Bhotes, or imagined or ideal Tibetans, in the middle of the hierarchy, provide the discourse through which the clothes are represented and consumed. Thus, the production and meaning of the Thamelcloth clothes is embedded in a long-standing hierarchical system of social organization. It is this, as we shall see, that provides the syntagmatic frame through which we can understand the relationship between clothing choice and identity in Nepal.

The last group of actors in this article and in the business are Europeans, the Tourists. When the caste system was created, most Europeans were "white," and they were designated a place in the caste system, even though very few had ever been inside Nepal. They were placed in the caste system next to the Muslims and along with the *Sudra*s (servants) at the very bottom of the hierarchy of *varna*s, only just above the untouchables, whom many consider non-human. Accordingly, the place of Europeans in this world-view was/is the opposite of where they generally placed themselves in "the great chain of being" (Lovejoy 1961 [1936])—that is, they are not at the top just below the angels. Prithvi Narayan Shah's vision of the state became formalized with a legal code in 1854, the *Muluki Ain*. In this code, Europeans were called *mlecch*, a Sanskrit term meaning "barbarian" or "pagan" (Hofer 1979:152). The new legal code specified rights, responsibilities, and penalties under the law according to caste. The code also specified rules for commensality and physical contact: a low-caste person's touching a high caste person was forbidden, for example, because of the "upward" transfer of less pure essential substances. The *Muluki Ain*, though no longer law, still lives on in practice, shaping social life in Nepal today.

In the social world of Nepal today, in which the categories of the *Muluki Ain* are both upheld and contested, and in which other forms of identity are being asserted and recognized (such as those of gender, class, and ethnicity) so too the identity "European" as conceived and placed in the *Muluki Ain* is also transforming, although vestiges of it still remain (as Hepburn 1997 elaborates). Even though included in the *Muluki Ain*, Europeans are not exactly like a Nepali caste proper. The code may have been instituted in the first place—ironically perhaps—as part of an effort to mark Nepal as uncontaminated by foreigners, a move at least in part inspired by awareness of the considerable number of British south of the border. Hofer suggests that the *Muluki Ain* might even have been ". . . a security screen against the outside world . . . [and] . . . demarcated the country's society against foreign societies and cultures by defining it as a specifically 'national' caste hierarchy" (Hofer 1979: 40). The *Muluki Ain* explicitly held that the Brahmins (high castes) "of the unsullied Hill Country," being untainted by the rule of foreigners (such as the British), were ". . . superior to the Brahmins of other countries and kingdoms" (Burghart 1984:117). So although Europeans were given a place in the caste-based code, their placement, at the bottom just above the untouchables along with other outsiders, is indicative of their status as defiling outsiders. Although they have caste-like qualities—the ability to pollute, to transfer their less pure essences to people of higher castes—they are not of a Nepali caste.

What is most pertinent here is that a "tourist" or a "European" is, like any other person in Nepal, viewed by many Nepalis in terms of a notion of personhood that entails ideas of caste/species; that is, a "tourist" or "European" is viewed in terms of discrete categories of "dividuals" sharing some essence, whose "individual" boundaries are not coterminous with the boundaries of the flesh as Westerners see it. Jang Bahadur Rana, a Nepali prime minister, traveled to Europe in the nineteenth century and carried a supply of Nepali water sufficient for the entire journey, so that while traveling he should not have to accept water touched by or offered by a European (Whelpton: 1983). That he was concerned with defiling himself by consuming something touched by someone ranked lower in the *Muluki Ain* indicates that he believed that Europeans, like Nepalis, were dividual—formed of a substance essence that could mix with other substances. In the late twentieth century, while doing research, this European herself ate meals with higher (than herself) caste Nepalis, in restaurants and homes, and was assured that this commensality was not a problem because a priest could always perform a purification rite. Although for some, Tourists might not be a Nepali caste, they are thought about in the logic that underlies the caste system.

The early Nepali state maintained an isolationist policy regarding "barbarians" and "pagans"; when Nepal was ruled by the Rana family for a century until 1951, the exclusionary policy became almost absolute. Except for a few British officials, non-Asian foreigners were denied entry; resident missionaries were deported; all newspapers and radios were banned. With the aid of the Indian Congress Party, the Ranas were overthrown in 1951 and Nepal began on a path towards opening to the non-Hindu world, which included allowing more diverse visitors, now grown to numbers sufficient to make the present tourist industry one of the mainstays of the Nepali economy.

## Consuming the Cloth of Barbaric Pagans

Although few Europeans were allowed to enter Nepal, the Rana rulers were greatly taken by European things, including fabrics and clothing. The Ranas ran Nepal like a vast feudal estate, appropriating labor and resources to enlarge and maintain their wealth, much of which they spent on lavish replications of material aspects of European life. Huge stucco palaces were built amongst the thatched huts, simpler brick structures, and pagoda temples in the Kathmandu Valley. Singha Durbar (the Lion's Palace), for example, was designed to resemble the Palace of Versailles in France, complete with mirrors, fountains, and over a thousand rooms. The materials for such a remarkable feat had, for the most part, to be carried overland over mountain passes, through malarial jungle, and across rivers, as there was at that time—by design, to keep out armies—no motorable road into Nepal.

Also carried over the rough terrain were European fabrics. Western-style clothing was first adopted for military dress. Bhim Sen Thapa led the Nepali government from 1806 to 1837, and he chose to wear entirely English dress (Chaudhuri 1960:168). He adopted for himself a Western military uniform, and ordered that his army be dressed in like fashion. Civilians, too, sought European fabrics, if not always European styles. An early British resident, granted permission to reside as a concession to continuing peace with India, was interested in promoting trade in European goods, and kept notes of what trade did occur. His accounts from 1830–31 show that European and Indian fabrics were imported and consumed by Nepalis in near equivalent amounts: velvet, cotton, broad-cloth, wool, satin, cambric, and chintz were popular, as was English lace. European imports also included cheap versions of Indian clothes, such as handkerchiefs and shawls, making these styles accessible to non-elites, or as Hodgson put it, the "lower orders" (Hodgson 1972 (1874): 105–8). As Liechty (1994: 537) notes, these foreign adornments came to mark and even define a person's class position in the hierarchy of Nepali society.

World-wide, variations in clothing can signify variations in status, sometimes encoded into law. In Japan, for example, during the Tokugawa period, spanning the seventeenth to the nineteenth centuries, laws specified which materials members of different social classes could use to make sandals (Roach and Eicher 1979: 13). In the sixteenth century Henry IV of France enacted laws restricting the use of silk to the aristocratic classes (Braudel 1981: 311). In like fashion, the Ranas, during their century ruling Nepal, enacted sumptuary laws that prohibited anyone other than the Rana elite from wearing European clothes; in so doing they maintained their own monopoly on the foreign fabrics that were markers of distinction. The Ranas, men and women, either wore completely Western outfits, or combined elements of these with South Asian clothing. Photographs of the Rana court show Rana women wearing hooped skirts and bustles under Western-style dresses (Shrestha 1986: plate 71; Sever 1993).

It cannot be inferred that because the Ranas emulated Western fashions, sartorial and otherwise, they no longer viewed Europeans as "barbarians" or "pagans." A recent conversation deprives me of that illusion. In 1993 a woman explained to me, in part, how it came to be that some Nepalis—even today—think that Tourists have tails, and thus are closely related to monkeys. She told me that the fact that Tourists have tails accounts for the peculiar protuberances built into European women's dress, as seen in photographs of the Rana period displayed around Kathmandu today. Bustles and hoops, in this understanding, were to accommodate tails, reflecting the codified understanding of Europeans in the great chain of being, that is, just above the (non-human) untouchables. Thus, although the Ranas certainly wished to wear and display European dress, we cannot assume that Europeanness, as some essential quality that constitutes the people of a caste, was sought after. Rather, it seems more likely that the Ranas wanted to be identified with some particular qualities the foreigners were seen to represent.

Nepali adoption of elements of Western dress, then, differed in extent and intent from the parallel process in India under the Raj. In India, the incorporation of European elements was, according to Tarlo's (1996) analysis, a compromise between dressing in a way that could increase a person's chance of being accepted by the British elite and yet maintaining the functionality and social markers important for continued interaction in the Indian climate and Indian society. In Nepal, on the other hand, the autocratic rulers were Nepalis, and they adopted European dress as markers to distinguish themselves from non-elites. The British made it difficult for Indians to emulate the dress of their rulers, the British elite, by developing ever more subtle and inviolable nuances of encoded meaning in dress, hard for Indians to read and emulate. The Nepali rulers made it hard for non-elites to dress just like them by simply prohibiting non-elites from purchasing or using European cloth and clothing.

The downfall of the Ranas in 1951 was spurred by the efforts of the Indian Congress Party, fueled, of course, by Western ideas of democracy. Thus began decades of political experimentation, the result of—and going hand in hand with—increased exposure to the ideas, things, and practices of the "barbaric pagans." The *mlecch* came as Peace Corps Volunteers, development workers, missionaries, mountain climbers, and occasionally just to visit; the *mlecch* brought a new system of medicine (at least in theory), and a new language (English) to be taught in schools which they set up for the elite of the land; they brought money in the form of development agency funding. Sumptuary laws were lifted, a motorable road to the south built, and trade increased. And Tourists, as tourists, eventually, began to arrive in large numbers: the barbaric pagans in a new guise. They came not as missionaries, doctors, or representatives of the British Government in India but as visitors, travelers, and explorers. Whatever the intentions of the tourists though, they were also Tourists, white Europeans (*mlecch*), marked as non-Hindu, as "other," bearing in and on their persons images of the world they came from. Increasingly, Nepali governments felt the need to at least be seen to be on the road to modernization and development, and so increasingly—through speeches, and eventually schools, radio, and billboards—the populace became aware of the idea of *bikas* (development, moving forward) as something that was perhaps imminent (Burghart 1984; Pigg 1992). Tourists, being from places of "lots of development" (*dherai bikas*), came to occupy an ambiguous place in the Nepali imagination, a place they still occupy today: they are in some sense people with essentially low-caste qualities, yet they are oddly wealthy and of high status (Hepburn 1994, 1997). They are much like the category known in the late Raj as the "India-returneds," people (Indians) who had been in Europe, and were therefore ritually defiled by contamination with the lower castes (all Europeans), but were, by having acquired the cultural capital (Bourdieu 1986) of European language, dress, and manners, of oddly high status (Tarlo 1996: 44 ). Whereas the Ranas could display cultural capital of the West on their persons and in their homes and keep the persons of the West on a distant horizon, today the products of the West are displayed, worn, and consumed in a context where images and people of the West are all around on the horizon—just outside the door in fact. They are worn in a context where Tourists, an ethnic group imaginatively and substantively linked with modernity, development, and democracy, as these are variously conceived, are an established part of the social landscape, not residents of a distant land. They are part of the world Nepalis look out on, and orientate themselves within, when they engage in sartorial choices.

## Aside from Thamelcloth: Clothing the Social Landscape of Nepal

Thamelcloth is based on a Himalayan design, approximating to one that was certainly used in Bhutan in the nineteenth century, as seen in court photographs of that period, but is just as certainly no longer pervasively worn in other than the contexts described here. The bolts of cloth are today woven in the mills of India, far from the Tourists' imaginings. They are shipped to Nepal and sold in the markets around Tahity Tol, a busy intersection in the old core of Kathmandu. Thamelcloth is made into clothing in the garment factories scattered around the Kathmandu Valley, and also produced as piecework in homes. The factory owners are, as far as I found out, from India, or are members of the Newar caste, ranked highly as *Vaisya*s (merchants) in the caste system.

In Kathmandu I lived next to a garment factory that produced shorts, skirts, and pants to be shipped overseas, and along with these orders, the Thamelcloth clothing would be sewn. Although this living situation was fortunate for research, it was unfortunate for getting enough sleep at times, as the workers, paid by the piece, arose at 4.00 a.m. in the sheds next to the factory—always to the accompaniment of Hindi film soundtrack cassettes—after having sewn until midnight the night before. Though the factory was well-lit and well-ventilated, the words "sweat-shop" and "exploited labor" would come to mind as I heard the drone of the machines begin, my irritation at the racket soberly tempered by gratitude that I did not have to join them. Whenever a rush order was completed, the people taking respite on the roof were Madeshi (Indian or Hindus from the South of Nepal) and Sarki (low-caste Hindus), and mostly men; the songs the people sang were Nepali. There were no Tibetans.

The Thamelcloth clothing designs are loose approximations to styles of clothing worn in Nepal. The linguistic and cultural diversity of Nepal reflects the long history of successive waves of migration through the Himalayas, as does, likewise, the tremendous array of clothing to be found throughout the country. The entry of Tourists, even the settling of some of them, and their influence on Nepali dress as related above, are just another addition to a long process of change and differentiation; the addition of new styles from the West, the world of Tourists, is part of an ongoing process of change. To understand how the Thamelcloth clothes are related to other styles of dress in Nepal, and how and why they are worn, requires seeing them in the context of these other styles, an overview of which I now turn to. Labeling the styles worn is in part arbitrary, and in part artificial. These styles are not fixed: they are particular combinations worn at a particular point in time, to express, as all clothing does, forms of social identity. Even in a country as small as Nepal I ran into the same problems as Tarlo (1996) in her overview of the entire subcontinent, and that is that names given to garments vary from region to region, and from language to language (as elaborated on by Ghuyre 1973; Chandra 1973; Goswamy 1993). Throughout I use the terms most commonly used in the Kathmandu Valley of Nepal.

In the north of Nepal, the strong influence of Greater Tibetan culture is readily apparent in language, culture and dress. Women usually still wear *chubba*s, long tunics that cross over at the front, and tie behind, and are held secure by thick hand-woven sashes wound around the waist to form a supportive thick waistband. Woolens and hardy blends do for day to day use, rich brocades for special events. Men's dress is similar, but whereas most women today retain traditional dress, most men wear Western-style pants, and in some regions—particularly Solu Khumbu, visited by many mountaineers and trekking tourists—people sometimes joke that a down jacket and mountaineering boots are "traditional Sherpa dress." This tendency for women to maintain what is marked as traditional dress carries into other parts of Nepal, as it does in fact in many areas of the world.

Saris are worn by women of groups self-identifying as Hindu (that is, women of the Nepali high castes), but sari-wearing can mean much more than this. Given the unrelenting government portrayal of Hindu culture as advanced and superior to other cultures (including those linked to Buddhism and animism in Nepal), and given the conflation in government speeches, policies, and schools of the ideas of development (*bikas*) and Hindu culture, wearing saris is also marked as a "developed" cultural practice (Burghart 1984; Pigg 1990, 1992). A schoolteacher in a small town a few miles outside the Kathmandu Valley, for example, explained to me that she and her peers always wore saris because they were "developed" (*bikasit*). She framed her clothing choices within the national hierarchy of cultural value, and in so doing set herself, implicitly, apart from neighboring people whose clothing (and by implication, culture)— being the *chubba*s described above—she read as a sign with the connotation "backward" (*abikasit*). As a young women she wore what young girls do today, either school uniforms of skirt and blouse, or the *suruwaal kurta*, also known as *punjaabi*, which is a long tunic over loose pants with long shawl scarf draped around the shoulders and across the chest. In urban areas today, adult women often now wear the *punjaabi*, often in stylish versions from India, or at least modeled on these. Increasingly today in the city, young women are wearing dresses, and even and often pants and blouses. In general, in a time of rapid social change, the dress codes and how they are read are in perpetual motion. Different items of clothing in different contexts—even for the same person—alternately become signs of "tradition," "modernity," "development" (as a quality of a person), or "backwardness."

Clothing and other forms of adornment for women are also used to signify—and are read to imply—moral status. And when social norms are rapidly changing, women's sartorial choices are something they stake their reputation on. Many women in Nepal today, and certainly most in the past, had (at most) just a few sets of clothes, which served not only as protection from the elements, but also—through style and color—as markers of social (ethnic/caste) identification and status. Beyond clothing, jewelry serves a similar function. The most highly valued jewelry in the Kathmandu Valley is 22-carat gold necklaces, bangles, rings, earrings and nose-rings. Until about five years ago, ready-made jewelry was rare: people bought gold by weight and then paid a goldsmith to craft it into the chosen style. Gold is compared to "money in the bank," because in hard times it can always be resold by weight at the current market rate. Different styles are characteristic of particular caste groups: for example, Brahmin women might wear a nose-ring, whereas a Newar woman would not. But as well as indicating wealth and caste identification, adornment can express women's relationship to men. Bledsoe (1984), describing Newari women's adornment in the Kathmandu Valley in the 1980s, argues that a woman's adornment is a display of her relationship to society and to her male relatives. It is appropriate for a woman to receive gold jewelry at marriage, and even before, to indicate that she is of marriageable age. It is generally considered inappropriate for a woman to wear jewelry after her husband dies, except for modest pieces. Another striking example of adornment marking a woman's social status is the use of *sindar*, red powder, boldly tracing the center part of a woman's hair. This is first applied (largely by those self-identifying as Hindu), as part of the marriage ceremony, symbolizing (say some) loss of virginity, and thereafter is applied on a daily basis as a marker of married status. The power of this imagery is captured in a popular song, whose literally translated first line is "I don't know when, but I have blossomed like a rhododendron." The voice is of a young woman on the threshold of marriage, singing that she is like the (bright red) rhododendron that blooms from a place where a rock is split. For her wedding a Hindu woman is required, and thereafter permitted, to wear a red sari and red bangles, clothing not worn by unmarried women. This in turn is put aside after a husband dies, to be replaced by white clothes. In the past, and today for many, adornment signifies social status, and for women, their relationship towards men.

In this light, it is perhaps not surprising that when a woman adopts a new style of dress, she can be seen to be simultaneously challenging, or redefining her relationship to men, and by implication her moral status; she uses fashion to represent and enact the conflict, in Simmel's words, between "adaptation to society and individual departure from its demands" (1971: 295). Many women wear *punjaabi* outfits and even Western-style clothing before marriage, but afterwards this sometimes becomes problematic. Virilocal residence is practiced throughout most of Nepal—that is, upon marriage a woman takes up residence with her husband's family. And some women find that around their husband's kin they can only wear saris, whereas on return visits to their parents' home, they continue to enjoy wearing *punjaabi*, skirts and even jeans. Western clothing for women is linked to notions of Western sexuality, as represented in media, and inferred from the behavior and appearance of Tourists. Nepalis often describe the dress of Tourist women as "open," "immodest," or such that "everything can be seen." And Nepalis, in relating their views of Tourists, often comment on their "shameless" behavior, which can include men and women holding hands, kissing, or touching in public, behavior that is taboo in Nepal. People have easy access to a wide range of pornographic films, which many take to be ethnographic. One Nepali woman told me that she believed Tourists did all the things she had seen in films, because of their "shameless" behavior in the streets. As she put it: "If they would hold hands and kiss *in front of their parents*, we can believe they would do anything when they were alone." Western clothing for women and men signifies an orientation toward modern sophistication; for women, however, it also signifies potential, if not actual, promiscuity. Women are often quite conscious that in wearing such clothes they are signifying identification with values that are in opposition to the role their husbands' kin would prefer them to play, that is, the role of the deferential wife, the embodiment of *laj* (that is, shame and modesty). For centuries in the Hindu world (Leslie 1992), much as in Mediterranean "honor–shame" societies (Campbell 1964; Sabbah 1984; Bridgwood 1995), a women's dress—modest or otherwise—has affected the reputation of her family. If she wears Western "immodest" dress around her husband's family, she feels, as one woman put it, that "Everyone will think I do things like Tourists do." If she wants to play other than a traditional role, then, a young woman walks a fine line in demonstrating her status through clothing: she might want to be seen to be *bikasit* (developed), but must be careful not to "do fashion"[2] excessively and thereby compromise her reputation.

In this way, Nepali women's clothing choices can alternately challenge social and political norms and uphold them (Hebdige 1979; Bean 1989). They can also, as Tarlo (1996:17) points out for clothing in general, alternately conceal identities and reveal them (Lurie 1992; Schneider and Weiner 1989)—or, I would say, at different times be signs of the various identities these women embody and negotiate, in different places, and through time. Although the media are certainly a rich source of images of the West, Tourists themselves are also messengers and embodiments of the West, in sartorial as well as other matters. When young men follow the Western media, watch Tourists, and adopt their styles, the line they walk is far broader than the women's, and traces different contours in the local moral landscape—a point we'll return to later. My point here is that for individuals, transitions to new clothing styles are marked not only by concerns with tradition and modernity as such, but also by other concerns that are conceptually and historically linked to these: concerns with gender role expectations of the past and today, and consideration of competing social values, such as the value of shame and modesty (*laj*) versus the value of life outside the marital home. The signified of Western or modern clothing apparel is not always the Western world as such; rather, it is aspects of that world—ideas of development, the freedom to step out of traditional roles—variously appropriated in negotiation with already existing socially embedded frames of meaning.

My own sartorial experience during the time the Thamelcloth's popularity grew will show how swift these transitions have been in Nepal. I lived with a high-caste family during a three-month visit to Nepal in 1988, and that I wore skirts was seen to be somewhat shameful, so to the relief and pleasure of my landlord/hosts I asked their tailor to make me two *suruwaal kurta* ensembles. Returning in 1990 I wore these same outfits and was told the style was no longer appropriate. *Suruwaal kurta*s were "*Tik*" (okay), they were fashionable, but the style, as evaluated in terms of constantly changing distinctions that are part of the internal fashion system, was "old" (*purano*). Through the next three years I acquired a wardrobe of four stylish—that is, in "*aajha ko* fashion" (today's fashion)—*suruwaal kurta* ensembles for all occasions. This was judged entirely suitable for a woman of my age, unmarried, and Western. Wearing a sari on formal occasions would be appreciated, but as I was unmarried and Western, others concurred that this would be a bit "over" as a daily practice. For the same reasons that a married woman wears a sari—to express her status and indicate compliance with role expectations—I was encouraged not to wear one. I was a Tourist and acted as a *punjaabi*/ skirt-wearing woman did, not like a dutiful daughter-in-law, so I should dress the part. Returning in 1997, after an absence of four years, I felt distinctly demure as I walked down the streets of Kathmandu in my *punjaabi*—attire that was appropriate clothing just a few years before— side by side with young Nepali women wearing short skirts and tight T-shirts. Although these young women were by no means the norm for the nation, their casualness and comfort in this way of dress, not possible just a short time before, is indicative of the swift rate of change. Their clothing choices are a form of practice through which they define their position in a world where social categories and frames of reference are swiftly being redefined.

The Thamelcloth clothing styles are drawn in part from the styles described above, but also from the styles of rural areas, themselves the result—like modern urban fashion—of processes of change, and the borrowing and adaptation of styles from elsewhere. In villages throughout Nepal, in areas to the south of the highest ranges, women often wear a *lungi* or *sarong*, a length of cloth sewn into a tube shape which, stepped into and deftly folded, covers them gracefully from the waist to above the ankle. The garment, though judged "backwards" by sari-wearing women, is practical for farming. It is a striking garment, the fabric in most cases being from India, Indonesia, Thailand and even Brunei, most commonly in batik-like patterns. Women formerly wore homespun garments, and the gift of woven articles had played, and in some areas continues to play, a role in forming, maintaining, and expressing social relations (March 1984). But men serving in the Gurkha regiments of the British army, or in the Indian army, began to bring *lungi*s home as gifts: given the high status of serving in the army, these clothing tokens became markers of status, and through time wider accessibility made them the norm, and manufactured *lungi*s have all but replaced homespun garments in many areas. A woman wears a *cholaa* blouse with the *lungi*. Made of plain or patterned cotton, or velvet, the *cholaa* crosses at the front and is secured by multiple ties. The blouse is tightly fitted, but with underarm gussets to facilitate movement. A wide length of cloth a few meters long is wound around the waist, creating an effect that most Western women would not aim to emulate, but also a firm support for the back, helpful during heavy agricultural labor. There are many regional variations: some women wear headscarves that drape down the back, others hats, others T-shirts or blouses, and the colors and patterns of these can indicate group or regional identities.

Nepali men's wear—the last assemblage of garments that shapes the Thamelcloth clothing—is less varied. Aside from the areas linked with greater Tibetan culture, as described above, and the southern areas towards the Indian border where men often wear some version of a *sarong*, or *dhoti* (a length of cotton wrapped loosely around the waist and often secured by passing the end of the cloth between the legs, drawing the fabric up) men wear some combination of "Western" dress and Nepali national men's dress. The fundamental aspect of Nepali men's national dress is a long tunic much like a woman's *cholaa* blouse except that it is much looser and longer, reaching down over the thighs, worn over very baggy pants tied with a waist drawstring. Both of these garments are usually of a neutral color, such as beige, light brown, and sometimes gray, and occasionally blue. Over this men will often wear a Western-style suit vest—called an *eystercoat*—in a plain dark fabric. A shawl adds warmth in winter. The only headwear worn with this is a *topi*, a hat that rests high on the crown and comes to a low peak on top. The fabric is either a plain dark colour, most often black, or a brightly colored hand-woven cloth called *dhaka*, distinctive of Nepal, and now produced in colors in vogue in the West, for which export clothing and shawls are made, the shawls selling for about $600 in London last year. Despite the range of colors now produced for the foreign designer market, Nepali men—from villagers to government officials—usually limit their choices to either plain black or gray, or a narrow range of patterns composed of white, red, orange, green, and black. Men will often carry cloth bags, or manufactured plastic or canvas bags, called *jholaa*s, as do women. As in most parts of the world, these ensembles marked as traditional are being replaced, particularly by young men and in the city, by jeans and trousers, shirts and T-shirts—a point we'll return to shortly.

We are now in a position to see that the Thamelcloth clothing designs are, as we noted at the start of this section, loose approximations to some clothing items worn in Nepal. There is the flat hat, like but unlike the *topi* (the national hat). There is a vest, like the men's *eystercoat*. Pants and shorts, cut loose with a yoke at the waist, are like the style of *suruwaal* (the bottom half of a style of women's *suruwaal kurta/ punjaabi*). A blouse is, like a woman's *cholaa* except that it is cut loose with baggy sleeves. And there are backpacks and shoulder bags, like but unlike *jholaa*s. The clothing is made either entirely from the brightly colored Thamelcloth, or is made from a solid color, usually black, maroon, or dark green, with Thamelcloth trim. The *suruwaal*, for example, are often black, with the front of the yoke in the colored fabric. The Thamelcloth clothing, then, is constructed in designs that are drawn from the repertoire of most Nepali tailors. The Thamelcloth clothing is based on a wide range of styles of clothing worn in Nepal, styles that mark ethnicity, caste, and class; the clothing is also based on styles marked by gender in the Nepali world.

## Tourists Consuming Foreignness: The Appeal of Tibetanness and Being a Certain Kind of Person

Many stores in Thamel carry a large range of the Thamelcloth clothing. It covers storefronts, and hangs in racks that reach out into the street, sometimes making Thamel appear to be the sight of a "medieval festival," according to one Tourist. Some Tourists make a purchase, and their motives for buying range from the purely practical, to the desire to be a good tourist, to the romantic and altruistic. Some have just come from India to the south, where it is consistently warm, and they need some warm clothes to wear on the trek to Mount Everest: the pants fit the bill, and have the undeniable advantage of being available in sizes large enough for what in Nepali eyes is the monstrous Tourist's physique. Others— unable to read the local dress codes—do believe that they are wearing local dress. Says one not uncommonly motivated Tourist, "I like to fit in wherever I go, so I like to dress like the locals," and the hat, pants, whatever, are added to their *mélange* of ethnic and national markers— bits and pieces from Indonesia and Rajasthan, and wherever else they have traveled in Asia. In this way tourists with various motives come to wear the Thamelcloth "range."

So some Tourists buy for practical reasons, and others with a generic notion of Nepali/Tibetanness that they are "fitting in" with. Other Tourists are attracted to these commodities with an intention that is altruistic, romantic, or "politically correct" as well as practical, namely to "help the Tibetan refugees." Asking tourists in the resort town of Pokhara about the souvenirs they had bought and why, many expressed this wish to help Tibetans by buying something thought to be linked to Tibetan culture, whether through its form or through contact with actual Tibetans. This is certainly how the Thamelcloth clothes—again, like other souvenirs—are presented by the primarily Newari and Kashmiri store-owners: "Tibetan hats," "Made by Tibetans," "Hand-made by Tibetans," they call out to the passing Tourists, and to what they know to be the Tourists' imaginal weakness. The only variation from this that I have heard is in response to a Tourist's direct question, "Which tribes wear these clothes?" "Nepali hill-tribes," was the answer, a response pre-sumably derived from the touristic fame of the Thailand hill-tribes, and a response evoked by the dress of these particular tourists, who were wearing "Thai Hill-Tribe" woven goods. But in general, people adhere to the time-tested practice of invoking the word "Tibetan"—something like a *mantra*—in order to make a sale.

Refugees from Tibet form a small part of Nepal's population, but to the Tourist they are highly visible and sought after. In the presence of Tibetans, other castes become all but invisible, a situation all are aware of. Says one Nepali resident of an area where Tibetans live alongside Nepalis:

> "I don't know why it is. If you have a room, and you tell the Tourist, 'This person is a Tibetan, and this person is a Tamang' (a caste/ethnic group living throughout the mid-hills of Nepal), they will always be more interested in talking to the Tibetan. I don't know why this is. They have some kind of power."

Tibetans know this too, and invoke the same sales mantra as the Nepali salesmen. Again, by the lakeside in Pokhara, a Tibetan cycles by, and softly says to me and other Tourists: "I am from Tibet, I have many somethings [sic]" [for sale]. So well is this sales pitch known that people even joke about it. A merchant from the Terai (south Nepal), with his Chinese and Indian goods set out on a platform next to the stupa, held up an Elvis T-shirt, made in India, and called out to me smirking: "Come on sister, good T-shirt. . . . From Tibet!"; and he waggled his head, laughing. He knows that I know, that we both know, that Tourists are attracted to anything from Tibet.

Most Nepalis do not share this fascination, and are somewhat per-plexed by the narrowness of the Tourist vision of the people of Nepal. For example, commenting on the danger of being in Boudhnath—an area with many Tibetans—at night, an elderly low-caste Nepali woman tells me: "Oh, those Bhote (colloquial in this case for Tibetans only), how they drink and how they fight, but oh, how Tourists love them." Many other Nepalis do not love them either, and—especially Hindus who attend the temple Pashupathinath—are concerned mostly that the Bagmati River, which flows by Boudhnath and then through the temple complex, carries the bodily wastes of these low-status beef-eaters into the areas Hindus ritually bathe and purify themselves in. In sum, the relationship between Tibetans and Nepalis is in many cases one of mutual antipathy—yet another point we shall return to shortly.

This linking in the imagination of the Thamelcloth clothing with "Tibetan refugees" persists across the Pacific. In a shopping mall in Calgary, Canada, an electrician sporting one of these hats with his coveralls and plaid shirt told me that his hat was "From Tibet, made by Tibetan refugees." And the hats, at that time—the summer of 1991— had become something of a fashion on the University of Calgary campus. The hats were, again, the students told me, "To support the Tibetan refugees." In one exceptional case a student offered that his purchase of the hat was to help people in Central America. The geographical dislocation, combined with the vagueness of the reference to a very complex political region, serves to emphasize the altruistic motive behind the purchase, although the carrying through is perhaps naive. Given that, through dress, people make a presentation to the world of how they would like to be viewed, we could say that not only do these people want to help the refugees, they also want to be seen to be the kind of person who does. The clothes become symbols through which people lead others to make assumptions about their motivations and actions, however imprecisely linked to actual effects in the world.

But what is wrong with this picture in the minds of well-intentioned consumers? Of course, Tibetans rarely make the clothes, sell the clothes, or even wear the clothes. Most of the Thamelcloth clothing is made in factories like the one I lived next to, staffed by Hindu low-caste tailors, and migrants from India. The salesmen, in Nepal and presumably in North America too, embellish an image that is already in the minds of the potential consumer: they produce an image of the goods, and of the Tibetans, as many Tourists would like to think of them, and as many Tourists would like to think of helping them. The Tourists are identifying with something they imagine about generic Tibetanness, but also with some Western idea of Human Rights and how refugees should be helped, and with their own particular ideas of what labor should be in an ideal society.

So beyond their practical reasons for buying, Tourists—both those visiting Nepal and those living in North America—are consuming an image of Tibetanness, and to a lesser degree Nepaliness; they are also consuming an image of what their relationship to Tibetans and Nepalis (the people and the cultures) is, or what they think it should be.

## Nepalis Consuming Foreignness Once Again: Being Modern in a Caste Society

As I said at the outset, over the past few years some Nepalis have taken to wearing the Thamelcloth clothes. Why do they wear them? "Helping the Tibetan refugees" is the furthest thing from their minds, and probably a motive they would scoff at. Remember, these are primarily high-caste young men under 25, who in general hold themselves to be of higher status than Tibetans, classified in the *Muluki Ain* legal code as Bhote, impure beef-eaters, and ranked quite low on the scale of social value (but above the barbarian, pagan Europeans). As we have seen, clothing is a marker of social status, and it would be very surprising if these young men wore this clothing because they wanted culturally, or politically, to align them- selves with Tibetans. These young Nepalis are selective in what they wear. For them the days of wearing the national two-piece men's costume are past. They wear made-in-the-East (Hong Kong and Thailand) Western- style clothes, imitating brand names such as Levi pants, Nike runners, Ralph Lauren shirts and T-shirts, often emblazoned with nonsensical English-language phrases, to convey further—to their chosen audience— the wearer's identification with the world of English-speakers; or, perhaps, at least their identification with the segment of Nepali society that appro- priates the goods and symbols of the West as part of its self-identification as *bikasit* (that is modern, developed) people. These young men call this "international style." They don't wear *topis* like their fathers. If anything, they wear a baseball cap (turned backwards, like white American men copying the style of black American men). A Jansport copy backpack completes the preferred look of the young men on the campus or in the places young men gather today.

Yet it is these young men who have started, over the past five years, to wear the Thamelcloth Tibetanesque clothes (Figure 4). And here too, they are selective. Not for them the baggy pants and tops, which perhaps look too much like women's styles as worn in Nepal. They read the gender markers unrecognized by Tourists: women wear *kurta*s, men don't. They also avoid the baggy pants, as these are seen by some to be "old fashioned," and they even laugh at the paradox that Tourists—otherwise in the forefront of "fashion"—wear a particular style (baggy pants) that they associate with the past. And not for them the shorts, the mark of a low-status laborer in Nepal.

They wear some combination of the following three Thamelcloth items with their international clothing: the vest, the hat, and the backpack. These three items are the closest to male traditional dress in Nepal—the *eystercoat*, the *topi* and the *jholaa*. Although they won't wear the *dhaka* cloth *topi*, or the ubiquitous gray or black vest, as their elders do, these young men will wear them in the Thamelcloth versions. What these young men reject is as important as what they select. Although male Tourists wear pants that resemble old-fashioned Nepali men's pants, or women's

**Figure 4**
A young Nepali man (center) wears a Thamelcloth vest while checking voter registration in Nepal's national election.

*suruwaal*, the young Nepali men reject these crossings over into the symbolic markers of female gender and elder males. Yet, to return to our question, why then do they wear clothes which from the Tourists' point of view are marked as "traditional"? And again, given that these clothes are constructed to appear "Tibetan," why would high-caste Hindu men appropriate them, given their higher status within the caste system and general distaste for things Tibetan shared with many other Nepalis? Why do they wear these Thamelcloth clothes, while shunning Nepali national costume, and otherwise dressing in what they call the "international" style?

It is because what the Tourist reads as "Nepali" or more usually "Tibetan," these young men read as "Modern." "Why do you wear these?" I asked. "*Aadhunik hune*"—to be modern—or "For fashion"—and commonly "Because we like European things." Tourists are seen to wear these clothes, and so the clothes are taken to be "modern"; just as Thamel is described by some Nepali people to be "Just like Europe," so the clothes sold and worn there are also taken, by some, to be European. However, it must be pointed out that although I asked over fifty young men why they wore the Thamelcloth clothing, not one said "To be like Tourists," or "To be like Europeans."

The Ranas by and large did not want to travel to Europe, and such a voyage was thought to entail great risk of contamination from the non-Hindu others, and low-caste *mlecch* barbarians were not welcome in Nepal: they did, however, want European things and wore them as signs of distinction. Times have changed, and many of the men wearing the Thamelcloth clothing would love to travel to Europe or America; caste taboos concerning commensal relations—between Nepalis, and between

Nepalis and foreigners—are not always so strictly observed; and today's government now posts signs at the airport such as "Welcome Tourists, our Honored Guests, our Gods." What has remained constant is the desire for Western goods, their consumption, and their display as signs of distinction.

In their motivations for wearing these clothes the young men are rooted within the Nepali world, but are orientating themselves to being modern, *Aadhunik* (from Sanskrit: "as things are now"). And as things are now, Nepal is in a time of rapid social transformation: the caste system remains in practice even as the political ideologies of equality and democracy and freedom are transforming the Nepali political landscape; the gender system persists despite women's rights movements; young men wear international style rather than the dress of their fathers, even though they expect to inherit their rightful place in the family hierarchy and wealth. And these transitions are expressed in the young men's adoption of the Thamelcloth clothing.

Calefato (1997: 70) suggests that "If clothing is a language, then fashion is a system of verbal and nonverbal signs through which this language expresses itself in the context of modernity." In Nepal in the past and today, clothing certainly was and is a language people speak to tell about their caste, class, and gender relative to other people. Through "doing fashion" today, Nepali people speak within this language, using its structures, to mark their multiple identities in changing times under the influence of, and incorporating, what is seen to be *bikasit* or *Aadhunik*. In the past in Nepal, Western clothing was worn to distinguish the Nepali elite through reference to the signs of a distant horizon. The Nepalis who today wear the Thamelcloth clothing (and the "international style") carry this horizon from the past, but integrate it with the horizon on their doorstep, a social landscape in which Tourists have a place along with other caste groups. Borrowing the vocabulary of Saussure (1974), this Nepali social landscape itself provides syntagmatic structures through which signs of clothing are read, indicating caste, status, and gender. The young Nepali men who wear the Thamelcloth clothing associate it not with "Tibetans," but with "Tourists," because when first seen the hats etc. (the signifiers) were worn by members of the Tourist caste (the signified). Associating the clothing with the Tourist caste, and aiming to encompass what the Tourist caste itself signifies (development, modernity, democracy), the Nepali wears it, as he might say, in order to "do fashion," to be modern, or because he likes European things. He reads Tourists and their clothing within the syntagmatic structure provided by the caste system, which posits essential qualities to caste groups. In doing so his clothing choices come to signify to himself and others (the signified) "*bikas*": he declares himself to have the qualities of a developed (*bikasit*) person.

But he is still Nepali: the declaration of *bikasit* identity is not abdication from other social identities. He chooses his Thamelcloth items according to the language of clothes that prefigured and co-exists with modernity. In choosing, he is mindful of markers of gender (shunning "female" items), age (shunning "old-fashioned" baggy pants), and status (choosing long pants, not shorts.) The chosen Thamelcloth clothes clearly fit paradigmatically within indigenous codes marking the oppositions male/female, modern/traditional, and high status/low status. And the young men unfailingly read these codes. They never wear the baggy pants, "female" items, or low-status shorts. If they did they would look inappropriately dressed. They also understand the social structure that underlies the code: for the Nepalis, the clothing is of necessity (given the logic of caste) sewn by low-caste, low-status people, whom the wearer (through identifying with high-status goods) raises himself above.

Tourists on the other hand do in a sense get it wrong—in Nepali terms—because they are reading by a different code altogether. For them, the Thamelcloth clothing signifies "Tibetanness" and "Nepaliness," with the connotation of "imbued with essence of the exotic other, and repressed refugees" and "labor supporting human rights." Whereas for Nepalis the Thamelcloth range is read on many levels, for the Tourist the entire range represents paradigmatically the first item in the following series of oppositions: Tibetans/non-Tibetans, human rights/human rights violations, dignified labor/exploited labor. The Tourist is also (ironically, perhaps, given the expressed motivation) blind to the underlying caste social structure that provides the labor. For the Tourist the clothing is seen to be the product of righteous labor that will help raise people from their unjustified low status, not the work of untouchables.

The Tourists and Nepalis are speaking different languages, yet, to carry the linguistic metaphor just a step further, they are indeed having a generative conversation. The Thamelcloth clothing would not exist without "Tibetanness," and Nepalis wouldn't wear them without having a conception of all the things and ideas that Tourists signify. Just as languages borrow and change, so too do cultures. In the late-twentieth-century world, there is, as Rosaldo puts it ". . . borrowing and lending across porous national and cultural boundaries . . ." (Rosaldo 1989: 217). In the language of clothes, Nepali people, and Tourists, speak of how they imagine themselves in the shifting social landscape that results from imaginative work in the borderzones they occupy together.

## Notes

1. The research on which this article is based took place between 1990 and 1993, and was generously funded by the following agencies: the United States National Science Foundation (Doctoral Improvement Grant N. BNS-9100365); the Joint Committee on South Asia of the Social Science Research Council and the American Council of Learned Societies, with funds provided by the Andrew W. Mellon Foundation;

the Social Sciences and Humanities Research Council of Canada; and the Cornell Graduate School and Center for International Studies. I thank them all for their support. For commentary on all or part of this article, thanks also to Bronwen Bledsoe, Kate Devine, John Forrester, Davydd Greenwood, Bernd Lambert, Judy Pettigrew, Kathy White, and participants in the Conference on South Asia, Madison, Wisconsin, Fall 1994.

2. The literal translation of the Nepali "Fashion *garnu*" is "to do fashion." The English word "fashion" is used with the Nepali "*garnu*" (to do) to create a verb, similar to the earliest uses in English of the word "fashion" as something that a person did, unlike the contemporary meaning of fashion as something a person wears. Barnard (1996: 7–9) traces such origins and variations in English usage.

## References

Barnard, Malcolm. 1996. *Fashion as Communication*. London: Routledge.

Bean, S. 1989. "Gandhi and Khadi: The Fabric of Independence." In *Cloth and Human Experience*, eds. A. Weiner and J. Schneider. Washington: Smithsonian Institute Press.

Bledsoe, Bronwen. 1984. "Jewelry and Personal Adornment Among the Newars." Report written for Year Abroad Program, University of Wisconsin, Madison.

Bourdieu, P. 1986. "The Forms of Capital." In *Handbook of Theory and Research for the Sociology of Education*, ed. by J. Richardson. New York: Greenwood

Braudel, Fernand. 1981. *Civilisation and Capitalism 15th–18th century. Vol. 1: The Structures of Everyday Life: The Limits of the Possible*. London: Collins.

Bridgwood, Ann. 1995. "Dancing the Jar: Girls' Dress at Turkish Cypriot Weddings." In *Dress and Ethnicity*, ed. J. B. Eicher. Oxford: Berg.

Burghart, Richard. 1984. "The Formation of the Concept of the Nation-State in Nepal." *Journal of Asian Studies* 44(1): 101–25.

Calefato, Patrizia. 1997. "Fashion and Worldliness: Language and Imagery of the Clothed Body." *Fashion Theory: The Journal of Dress, Body and Culture* 1(1): 69–90.

Campbell, John. 1964. *Honour, Family and Patronage: A Study of Institutions and Moral Values in a Greek Mountain Community*. Oxford: Oxford University Press.

Chandra, M. 1973. *Costumes and Textiles, Cosmetics and Coiffure in Ancient and Medieval India*. Delhi: Orient Longmans.

Chaudhuri, Kshitish, C. 1960. *Anglo-Nepalese Relations from the Earliest Times of British Rule in India till the Gurkha War*. Calcutta: Modern Book Agency.

Dumont, Louis. 1980. *Homo Hierarchicus: The Caste System and Its Implications*. Chicago: University of Chicago Press.

Ghurye, Govind S. 1951. *Indian Costume*. Bombay: Popular Book Depot.

Goswamy, B. N. 1993. *Indian Costumes in the Collection of the Calico Museum of Textiles*, Vol. 5. Ahmedabad: D. S. Mehta for the Calico Museum.

Hebdige, Dick. 1979. *Subculture: The Meaning of Style*. London: Methuen.

Hepburn, Sharon. 1994. "The Case of the Missing Trekker: Moral Geography and Miraculous Survival. And Rodney King." In *Anthropology of Nepal: Peoples, Problems and Processes*, ed. M. Allen. Kathmandu, Nepal: Mandala Book Point.

——. 1997. "To See the World: Vision, Tourism, Anthropological Practice, and Ethnic Politics in Nepal." Ph.D. thesis, Cornell University.

Hodgson, Brian H. 1972 [1874]. *Essays on the Languages, Literatures, and Religion of Nepal and Tibet, Together with Further Papers on the Geography, Ethnography, and Commerce of Those Countries*, Vol. 7, *Biblioteca Himalayica Series II*. New Delhi: Manjusri Publishing House.

Hofer, Andras. 1979. *The Caste Hierarchy and the State in Nepal: A Study of the Muluki Ain of 1854*. Innsbruck: Universitatsverlag Werner.

Leslie, Julia. 1992. "The Significance of Dress for the Orthodox Hindu Woman." In *Dress and Gender: Making and Meaning*, ed. Ruth Barnes and J. B. Eicher. Oxford: Berg.

Liechty, Mark. 1994. "Fashioning Modernity in Kathmandu: Mass Media, Consumer Culture, and the Middle Class in Nepal." Ph.D. thesis, University of Pennsylvania.

Lovejoy, Arthur O. 1961 [1936]. *The Great Chain of Being: A Study of the History of an Idea*. Cambridge, MA: Harvard University Press.

Lurie, Alison. 1992. *The Language of Clothes*. London: Bloomsbury.

March, Kathryn S. 1984. "Weaving, Writing, and Gender." *Man (N.S.)* 18(4): 729–44.

Marriott, McKim, and R. B. Inden. 1985 [1974]. "Social Stratification: Caste." In *Encyclopedia Britannica*.

Pigg, Stacey Leigh. 1990. "Disenchanting Shamans: Representations of Modernity and the Transformation of Healing in Nepal." Ph.D. thesis, Cornell University.

——. 1992. "Inventing Social Categories Through Place: Social Representations and Development in Nepal." *Comparative Studies in Society and History* 33(3): 491–513.

Roach, M. E., and J. B. Eicher. 1979. "The Language of Personal Adornment." In *The Fabrics of Culture*, ed. J. M. Cordwell and R. A. Schwarz. The Hague: Mouton.

Rosaldo, Renato. 1989. *Culture and Truth: The Remaking of Social Analysis*. Boston: Beacon Press.

Sabbah, Fatna. 1984. *Woman in the Muslim Unconscious*. Oxford: Pergamon.

Saussure, Ferdinand De. 1974. *Course in General Linguistics*. London: Fontana/Collins.

Schneider, Jane, and A. Weiner. 1989. "Introduction." In *Cloth and Human Experience*, eds. A. Weiner and J. Schneider. Washington, DC: Smithsonian Institution Press.

Sever, Adrian. 1993. *Nepal under the Ranas: Photographs from the Collection of Jharendra Shumsher Jang Bahadur Rana*. New Delhi: Oxford and IBH Pub. Co.

Shrestha, Padma Prakash. 1986. *Nepal Rediscovered: The Rana Court 1846–1951*. London: Serindia Publications.

Simmel, Georg. 1971. "Fashion." In *On Individuality and Social Forms*, ed. G. Wills and D. Midgley. Chicago: University of Chicago Press.

Smith, Valene (ed.). 1978. *Hosts and Guests: The Anthropology of Tourism*. Oxford: Basil Blackwell.

Stiller, Ludwig. 1973. *The Rise of the House of Gorkha: A Study in the Unification of Nepal, 1768–1816*. New Delhi: Manjushri.

Tarlo, Emma. 1996. *Clothing Matters: Dress and Identity in India*. Chicago: University of Chicago Press.

Whelpton, John. 1983. *Jang Bahadur in Europe: The First Nepalese Mission to the West*. Kathmandu, Nepal: Sahayogi Press.

*Fashion Theory*, Volume 4, Issue 3, pp.301–322
Reprints available directly from the Publishers.
Photocopying permitted by licence only.
© 2000 Berg. Printed in the United Kingdom.

# Ambivalence, and Its Relation to Fashion and the Body

**Anne Boultwood
and Robert Jerrard**

Anne Boultwood is a
psychologist and visiting
lecturer at the University of
Central England. Since 1997,
she has been researching into
the psychology of fashion, and
its relation to the body.

Dr. Robert Jerrard is Professor
of Design Studies in the School
of Design Research, Institute of
Art and Design, University of
Central England.

## Introduction

Both the body and fashion are independently related to self-awareness,
and the nature of their joint interaction suggests a relationship between
the two. Whilst the nature of such a relationship remains unclear, the
literature in both fields reveals potentially common themes. Body–fashion
interaction lends expression to the unconscious experience of self, both
internally as part of a "selfing" process, and externally by creating an
identity to present to others. Conflicts within the psyche, played out on
the body, contribute to a fragmented sense of self, and the view of fashion
as exacerbating its disintegration may be contrasted with the belief in

the power of fashion to integrate. The ambiguity of this internal conflict is echoed by the conflicting social-psychological needs of imitation/identification and differentiation that characterize the social experience of the body, and are manifested in the individual's response to fashion. The apparent superficiality of fashion is belied by its role in giving expression to the ambivalence derived from the internal conflict of the individual, and the external ambivalence of postmodern society. Individual ambivalence focuses on the concept of the ideal body, an image created by society for the objectified body to aspire to, and a platonic ideal that encapsulates the individual sense of embodiment. Fashion's aspirational role is to provide a means of creating an approximation to the ideal. This occurs at the body boundary, the threshold that marks the demarcation between self, as experienced within the body, and non-self as it impinges from without. The ambiguity of the body–clothing threshold fuels the fashion process, and it may be that body boundary represents an interface between the experience of self and its expression through fashion.

Both fashion and the body are areas of human interest concerned with image. Both also appear to address issues of self-awareness at some fundamental level. It therefore seems reasonable to assume a relationship between them, though the nature of that relationship remains unclear. At first sight, it appears that both are subject to similar influences, and it is possible that these common influences are in some way responsible for their interaction.

This article reviews a range of approaches to body and fashion. Its intention is to develop an integrated account of their relationship that avoids narrow interpretations based on binary oppositions. The authors acknowledge that many of these approaches, which focus on specific social and psychological conflicts, are necessarily expressed in binary terms, but hope to present a broad-based view of fashion and its wide-ranging contexts that recognizes the complexity of the relationship.

## Fashion/Body Themes

When fashion and the body are considered separately, three themes emerge that are common to both. As a first step in understanding their relationship, it may be useful to explore their interaction within the context of their common themes. These themes are made explicit in theories of fashion, and are implicit in much that has been written about the body, both in clothing and in psychological contexts. They are:

- the unconscious communication of the self
- the twin processes of imitation/identification and differentiation
- the concept of ambivalence.

The last of these, the experience of ambivalence, appears to be central to much of human self-awareness. It originates in the individual from internal, unconscious processes, and is fuelled by external, social experience. Thus, whilst each theme will be considered separately, their relation to the ambivalence of the individual will provide the focus for exploration.

### Communication of the Self

Bodily behavior is a central aspect of non-verbal communication. This includes the use of clothing and, by extension, fashion. However, to focus solely on its communication role is to disregard its other aspect as part of the experience of self-awareness. Radley (1991), for example, has argued that to restrict the role of the body solely to its capacity for communication is to ignore its broader impact as a cultural device in its own right. This view is shared by Baerveldt and Vostermans (1998), who have suggested that the self should be viewed more as a process than an entity, and the body as integral to that process. The construction of a self that is both social and personal, they describe as *selfing*; the body thus becomes a *selfing device*. According to this view, communication, rather than being the purpose of bodily behavior, may be seen almost as an expression of subjective bodily experience, both to the self and others.

This emphasis on communication has also encouraged the adoption of a linguistic analogy. Indeed, Harré and Gillett (1994) have argued that the body can best be understood within a linguistic framework; and both Barthes (1983) and Lurie (1992) have notably applied a linguistic analysis to fashion and clothing respectively. This view too has been criticized for its reductionism. Since both are forms of non-verbal behavior, their message is not only non-linguistic, but is also highly complex. Lurie (1992) argued that specific garments, for example a man's business suit, and specific colors, for example a fiery red, send specific messages; but what would the perceiver make of a man's red suit? Whilst Lurie herself would acknowledge the ambiguity, her semiotic approach somewhat simplifies the message. McCracken (1988) claimed that as an analogy language is inappropriate, since, unlike language, this message is not read from left to right and from the top of the page to the bottom, but rather is interpreted holistically, with all parts seen simultaneously. Clothing, like the body, is not in that sense a discursive medium; it is primarily visual, though it can also be tactile, and involve other senses. Bodily behavior— movement, gesture, posture, etc.—and clothing characteristics interact to produce a complexity of meaning, which both informs the process of *selfing* and communicates some measure of that self to others.

An example of the way in which the two work together is the occasion when the late Princess of Wales wore a famously sexy black dress on the night that her husband confessed publicly to adultery. The message, according to the press, was clear: how could any man be unfaithful to such a desirable woman? That, almost certainly, is the message that Princess Diana intended to convey; but there was another aspect to her look that evening. To go with the dress she wore a pair of very high stiletto heels—appropriate to the dress, and the sexy look, certainly, but the adoption of high heels was also part of her process of *selfing*. Because she was taller than her husband, the princess had traditionally worn flat or very low-heeled shoes; the high heels were part of the new, independent self that was developing, and that she chose to project from that moment.

The body–clothing communication is a *mélange* of multi-messages, which often contradict each other, creating ambiguity for both sender and receiver. Our perception of these messages, as McCracken (1988) has said, involves interpreting the whole appearance. The interaction of its parts influences our total assessment (Lennon and Miller, 1984–5), in order to create a *Gestalt* that is greater than their sum. The *Gestalt* is made up of shape, color, size, etc. of both body and clothing, of characteristics of clothing such as fashionability or elegance, and of the way the two work together. In creating a *look* the individual is creating a *Gestalt*, and by recombining the parts a new *Gestalt* may be created. Vivienne Westwood, for example, combines elements from the costume of different historical periods to conceive a new style. Thus, her *Pagan* look (1988) combined classical drapery with eighteenth century fullness to create a new *Gestalt* of her making. The consumer might have chosen to wear it, not with Westwood's high heels, but with flat boots, and so yet another *Gestalt* would have emerged.

The *look* we create is not a static entity, but, because it is non-discursive, it cannot evolve during interaction. Mistakes cannot be rectified, nor can we explain what we really meant (Kaiser 1997). This partly explains why *getting it wrong* can be so devastating. In *The New Dress* Virginia Woolf describes the feelings of her heroine, Mabel, who wished to be "not fashionable" but "original," when she discovers that the message she sent was not the one received.

> . . . she went straight to the far end of the room, to a shaded corner where a looking-glass hung and looked. No! It was not "right". And at once the misery which she always tried to hide, the profound dissatisfaction—the sense she had had, ever since she was a child, of being inferior to other people—set upon her, relentlessly, remorselessly, with an intensity which she could not beat off . . .

It is also unfocused. McCracken (1988) compares the body–clothing message to a *broadcast signal*; within a particular social context the message will be received by anyone who cares to interpret it, regardless of the intended audience. To be at the height of fashion, for example, gives a particular message; but only if those present are aware of fashion. If they are not, then their interpretation may be that the wearer is eccentric or ridiculous.

The message is highly complex and, though interpreted holistically, involves both body (attractiveness, size, gesture, posture) and clothing (color, shape, design) variables. It is hardly surprising, therefore, that it is rife with ambiguity. Indeed, F. Davis (1985) claims that ambiguity is its overriding characteristic.

It is apparent that this interpretation operates at a level beyond our conscious awareness, and it is possible that our self-awareness derives from the same source. The unconscious has been implicated in body awareness since the birth of psychoanalysis, and despite differences in interpretation, has continued to provide the focus of attention. At a time when Cartesian duality dominated scientific enquiry, Freud (1963) was the first to overlay body experience with that of the psyche, introducing the concept of the unconscious in the process. His belief in the unconscious as a morass of unresolved conflicts that are acted out on the body has provided the foundation of all subsequent psychoanalytic theories.

Lacan (1977) differed from Freud in his view of the body as representational, and his body as image is directly opposed to Freud's biological body. Nevertheless, body awareness remains central to his account of psychic development. Even Irigaray's (1985) radical rejection of both Freud's and Lacan's *malist* sexuality retains that sexuality as the core of her own feminist account.

In psychoanalytic accounts of fashion, clothing is seen as a means of addressing psychic conflicts that are acted out on the body. Fashion, though it is an aspect of clothing, is seen as a vehicle for bodily reconciliation of conflict. It is almost as though, in our unconscious awareness, the two have become inextricably intertwined. For Flügel (1930), the modesty/eroticism conflict that characterizes fashion is played out on our clothing, not as external symbols, but rather as part of ourselves, in the same way as Freud's (1963) neurotic symptoms. Creation of the self, it seems, may be achieved through the body or clothing. Similarly, König (1973) believed that fashion's primary purpose is to address the conflict between *deathwish* and awareness of our own mortality: a mortality epitomized by the aging body.

According to these psychoanalytic accounts, the unconscious is full of negative conflicts that are acted out on the body, either directly or by means of fashion. Implicit in this view is a somewhat grim, *angst*-ridden view of human self-awareness. It is hard to reconcile this depressing view with the creativity of fashion. Schiaparelli's surrealist designs, for example, were related to this psychoanalytic view; yet what could be more fun and fantastical than a hat that looked like a shoe? Similarly, body awareness, if it were solely the site of internal conflict, would be a wholly negative experience, and this clearly is not the case. The significance of these theories, however, lies in their articulation of the role of fashion in expressing the unconscious within the parameters of the body–clothing interaction.

A possible exception to the body–clothing link is the work of Adorno (1967), who sees fashion as subverting the individual consciousness. It should be noted, however, that Adorno's psychoanalysis is rooted in the oedipal conflict, and is therefore implicitly bound up with body awareness. Lacan (1977), of course, also viewed fashion as a threat to the self; but unlike Adorno, he did not see this as something being visited on the individual by society. For Lacan, the individual is a willing participant, driven by the need for integration. The body as image is central to this need, and clothing is a way of achieving this. The drive towards integration, therefore, creates the need for novelty implicit in fashion. However, fashion seeks to mould the body into its own image. The individual, rather than using fashion, is used by it, and fashion ultimately fails.

Wilson (1985) shares Lacan's belief in a fragmented self, but takes the opposite view of fashion. She believes that fashion acts to "glue" together this fragmentary self into *the semblance of a unified identity*. Wilson would agree with Lacan that the desires of the unconscious are unfulfillable; where she differs is in her essentially creative view of fashion as a fantasy vehicle that allows us to play out those desires.

Both Wilson (1985) and Kaiser (1997) have drawn attention to the ambivalence that pervades all these accounts; and Kaiser has pointed to their contribution to fashion theory by highlighting the role of unconscious motivation. Clearly, whether or not we acknowledge the existence of an unconscious as a psychic entity, in our experience of the self we are influenced by something that operates at a level beyond our conscious awareness, and it is possible that we use both body and fashion to give this experience expression (Wilson 1985). This involves both internal and external aspects (Table 1), as experience of self is translated into expression of self.

**Table 1**  The Role of Fashion and the Body in the Expression of Self-awareness

| Internal Role | External Role |
| --- | --- |
| experiential | expression |
| *selfing* | identity |

### The Role of Identification and Differentiation

The opposing processes of identification and differentiation are implicated in our sense of self and also in our interaction with others. The concept of identification describes our psychological need to belong, whilst that of differentiation describes the equally powerful need to feel unique (Kaiser 1997). The conflict between the two colors much of both our social and our personal life, and was first identified by Simmel (1904) as the major force driving fashion change.

The concept of identification was originally proposed by Freud (1963) as the resolution of his *Oedipus complex*, but was subsequently taken up by social learning theorists and implicated in the socialization process. According to social learning theory, behavior is first learnt by the process of imitation, and is internalized through identification (Bandura 1977). Whereas imitation involves the acquisition of specific behaviors, identification involves the generalized adoption of not only the behavior, but also the beliefs, values, attitudes, etc. of significant others, for example parents. These processes continue into adulthood and fuel group dynamics. We adopt behavior appropriate to a group and then internalize the associated beliefs. Since beliefs are inferred from behavior, the corollary of this process is that we choose to identify with those whose behavior appears similar to ours. This is particularly true of appearance aspects of behavior, since these represent our first assessment of others. There is evidence that we are attracted to those who look similar to ourselves (Stone 1965), and Berscheid and Walster (1974) demonstrated that we select partners who are at a similar level of attractiveness. Berscheid *et al.* (1971) showed that the same is true for same-sex friendships. The way we dress appears to have similar effects. We are more likely to help those who dress similarly (Feldman 1972), and more likely to be attracted to them (Buckley 1983).

Closely related to this need for identification is the concept of conformity, which leads us to alter both behavior and beliefs in response to perceived group pressure (Asch 1956). Both identification and conformity involve the internalization of group beliefs and attitudes, and it is not surprising that we feel pressure to conform in our clothing choice (Gurel *et al.* 1972). Snyder and Fromkin (1980) have pointed out that similarity in clothing lends cohesiveness within a group by uniting the members and segregating them from others, and conformity in dress is certainly conducive to group acceptance (Creekmore 1980). One of the functions of fashion, then, may be to cement that sense of cohesiveness.

Alongside our need to belong is the equally powerful need to see ourselves as unique; this is the concept of differentiation. The feeling of being unique supports our sense of self, and the fact that physically we are unique reinforces that feeling. Body awareness provides a focus for differentiation, and the need to maintain uniqueness translates into our feelings about clothes (Snyder and Fromkin 1980). Wilson (1985) has suggested that this need for individualism has been promoted by the growth of city life, and that fashion is one adjunct of this. Increased interaction with strangers led to feelings of confusion. Fashion, by allowing the individual to manipulate the self, provides the means of distinguishing oneself from others. One of the significant aspects of fashion in our post-industrial society is the speed of fashion diffusion. It is suggested that this is a result of faster and more global communication; it may also be a function of the increased need for individualism.

Snyder and Fromkin (1980) proposed a theory of uniqueness in which individuals vary in the extent of the differentiation that they need. No one wants to feel completely different, since this would inevitably lead to isolation from the group. It is rather a need to have a sense of being different. However, when the degree of similarity becomes too high, the negative affective response we experience leads us to re-establish our differentiation. We use consumer items such as clothing to emphasize the difference, and this is what fuels the fashion process. Snyder and Fromkin have suggested that the reason we value our clothing is because of its uniqueness. In *Wild Swans* Jung Chang describes how people would use ribbons or other accessories to individualize their Mao suits. Even in the early days of the revolution, her mother risked severe reprimand when she and a friend made pink blouses. "Next day they wore them under their Lenin jackets. My mother turned her pink collar out and spent the whole day feeling terribly excited and nervous. Mrs Ting was even more daring, she not only turned her collar outside her uniform, but rolled up her sleeves so that a broad band of pink showed." Toffler (1980) has similarly suggested that the recent mass customization of clothing production has been so successful because of the fact that it facilitates the making of our clothes unique.

The forces of imitation and differentiation, according to King (1963), are at the root of this *simultaneous adoption* process of fashion change, with fashion innovators constantly seeking differentiation and fashion followers imitating them. The force of conformity makes it difficult for innovators to deviate too much from the norm, unless they wish to step outside the group into a subculture (Hebdige 1979). Harman (1985) calls this *acceptable deviance*: individuals will deviate enough to be unique, but will conform sufficiently to be accepted. This works at both ends of the spectrum: it is as unacceptable to be strikingly unfashionable as it is to be outrageously fashionable. In our striving to fulfill both needs, we are driven to seek a compromise. Paradoxically, what we achieve is mediocrity. The attempt to cope with these conflicting drives creates a sense of ambivalence within us that F. Davis (1985) has suggested reflects the ambivalence that characterizes much of our present social milieu, which, he claims, provides the driving force behind fashion change.

## Ambivalence

The conflicting, sometimes contradictory, attitudes that characterize much of our emotional and psychological experience are encapsulated in the concept of ambivalence. It is a concept that pervades our late-twentieth-century cultural and personal experience. Cultural ambivalence is apparent in the meeting of different cultures: ideas are borrowed, and recycled in the arts, philosophy, and lifestyles; yet at the same time there is a need to maintain cultural identity (Kaiser 1997).

The same process affects our individual sense of identity. Fred Davis (1992) has argued that individual identity develops out of culturally determined formulae, for example, masculine–feminine, youth–age, work–play, etc. These formulae are characterized by conflict, and their interplay within the individual creates identity ambivalences that pervade society.

Wilson (1985) believes that there is a deep-rooted ambivalence in society that manifests itself in all areas of human endeavor, including politics, the arts and fashion. This may be exemplified by the work of the Japanese artist Mariko Mori. An ex-model, she turned to art to escape being treated as a "doll" by the fashion industry. In creating her art, an eclectic mix of fashion imagery, pop culture and traditional Buddhist philosophy, she uses her own body, and the impression created is very much that of a "doll." She employs a team of stylists, make-up artists, photographers and lighting technicians, so that her work resembles a fashion shoot.

It has been suggested that this ambivalence, so characteristic of postmodern society, is in fact created by the postmodern experience. Baudrillard (1981) sees it as the principle of symbolic exchange, created by the ultraconsumerism of our capitalist society. However, it could be argued that ambivalence has always formed part of our psychological make-up. The forces of identification and differentiation are not merely a symptom of postmodernism, but appear to be fundamental to the human psyche, creating ambivalence throughout the developmental process. It is particularly striking during adolescence, but Blos (1967) has argued that adolescent ambivalence is a resurgence of that experienced at around three years old, and is part of the individuation process. Recent work on adult development has identified similar feelings at the time of the so-called *mid-life crisis* (Sheehy 1976).

The discomfort we feel is related to our psychological need for consonance. Festinger's *cognitive dissonance theory* (1957) argues that when two cognitions, held simultaneously, are psychologically inconsistent, the resultant tension drives us to alter our cognition to achieve consistency. Typically, this takes the form of a change in attitude, and involves some rationalization. Our feelings of ambivalence at critical periods in our development are resolved by the adoption of a rationale that allows us to reconcile our opposing needs for identification and differentiation, and provides us with an acceptable perception of the self.

The ambivalence that surrounds the body is related to self-perception, and can be summarized by Turner's (1984) assertion that we both *have* and *are* bodies. This is the difference between body as object, known and understood as an entity separate from the self, and the concept of embodiment in which the body becomes fundamental to self-awareness. Radley (1998) claims that embodiment is central to our socio-psychological life because of its capacity for symbolizing. The body may be said to be transformed into a *stylized body* (Goffman 1971) which represents the character of the body in the sense that Simmel (1991) speaks of style. Radley's body is similar to Lacan's (1977) representation of a body. There is an ambiguity in this view, which, while acknowledging the centrality of the body, also seeks to render it ethereal, and possibly harks back to the *mind over matter* male view of self-awareness.

For many feminists (for example, Irigaray 1985) embodiment is more rooted in the physicality of the body, and is seen in the light of female emancipation. However, this view of the body must be contrasted with the objectification of the female body. According to Berger (1972), a woman perceives herself through the eyes of a man, and judges herself accordingly. Berger intended this as a criticism of women; but feminists have since adopted it as a way of explaining women's objectification. The tendency of women to view their bodies as though through the eyes of a third person was demonstrated in a recent study (Frederickson *et al.* (1998)) in which women's mental capacity was undermined by wearing a swimsuit. Even though they were alone, it seems that the women were so preoccupied with the image they presented they were unable to concentrate on solving mathematical problems. This was not the case for men. Despite the feminist shift from body as object to body as subject, this ambiguity still prevails, and results in women's ambivalence towards their bodies. The object body could be viewed as the body's external aspect; and it is this aspect that is compared to the ideal body.

The pursuit of the ideal, which in our present culture is one of thinness, has been blamed on media images, particularly those contained in fashion magazines. If women do not conform to the ideal of beauty presented by the media, they feel alienated. It is possible, however, that the media reflect an obsession that already exists, and influences our assessment of each other (Adams and Crane 1980). Physical attractiveness is associated with a host of other positive qualities (Dion *et al.* 1972). Attractive people therefore have an advantage in their interaction with others. For women, however, beauty can be a double-edged sword. Women achieve status through beauty, yet it can also make others suspicious of their motives (Sigall and Ostrove 1975).

The cultural ambivalence towards beauty is echoed by that towards aging. Just as the male *gaze* objectifies woman, so its withdrawal can render her invisible (Greer 1999). For women the loss of beauty and youthfulness (and in our culture, the two are normally synonymous) can lead to a loss of self-definition. There is great pressure on women to retain their youthfulness, yet in doing so they risk the ridicule of society (Wilson 1985). On the one hand, both cosmetics and the development of cosmetic surgery have provided women with the means to recapture youth and beauty; on the other, they face society's disapproval for their lack of dignity if they are seen to resort to these methods. On a personal level, there is the ambivalence of reconciling the desire to retain what has been a source of status with the desire to be recognized for achievement rather than appearance.

Fashion is also characterized by ambivalence, but this may also be the expression of something that already existed. Baudrillard (1981:51) said that fashion: "embodies a compromise between the need to innovate and the other need to change nothing . . ." His is a nihilistic view of fashion, but he recognized the "ambivalence . . . of contradictory and irreconcilable desires, inscribed in the human psyche . . ." (Wilson 1985: 246). Baudrillard also recognized the tensions that create fashion: the desire for novelty, to distinguish oneself, opposed by the need to keep things the same, to conform. This conflict creates the ambivalence that Baudrillard claims is the foundation of all modern culture, and that is manifested in fashion in different ways. Similarly, F. Davis (1985) has argued that the identity ambivalences that characterize society are experienced, to a greater or lesser extent, by all individuals, and will find expression through fashion. Ambivalence, in one form or another, has been cited by many theorists as a crucial aspect of fashion: some explicitly (Baudrillard 1981; F. Davis 1985; Kaiser, Nagasawa and Hutton 1995), others by implication (Lurie 1992; Simmel 1904; Blumer 1969, for example). Table 2 summarizes these views, and it can be seen from this, that, while these theorists may differ in their accounts of the nature of ambivalence, they agree on the fundamental process. Ambivalence in the individual seems to derive both from internal conflict and from the external social milieu; fashion apparently gives expression to ambivalence and provides a tool for coping with conflict.

Our ambivalence towards fashion reflects the ambivalence we feel towards the body. Both appear to be a manifestation of the inner conflicts of the psyche, and the nature of the ambivalence in both cases is the same. This suggests that they are in some way interrelated, and that their coincidence is more than mere coincidence.

**Table 2** Ambivalence in the Individual, and Its Relation to Fashion

| Theorist | Nature of Ambivalence | Function of Fashion |
| --- | --- | --- |
| Simmel (1904) | identification/differentiation | reconciliation |
| Flügel (1930) | modesty/eroticism | reconciliation |
| King (1963) | imitation/differentiation | expression |
| Blumer (1969) | past/future | coping mechanism |
| König (1973) | *"deathwish"*/mortality | defence mechanism |
| Hebdige (1979) | rebellion/belonging | expression |
| Lurie (1992) | feminist expression/female oppression | expression |
| Baudrillard (1981) | cultural ambivalence | expression |
| Wilson (1985) | cultural ambivalence | expression |
| F. Davis (1985) | identity ambivalences | expression |
| Kaiser, Nagasawa and Hutton (1995) | cultural ambivalence | experimentation and negotiation |

Fashion appears to be superficial, yet Wilson (1985) has pointed out that it has a depth that echoes the depth of human self-awareness. This may be because fashion is the cultural sign of fundamental inner conflicts, as described by psychoanalytic theorists (for example, Flügel 1930). Certainly, its importance to the individual is reflected in the profitability of the fashion industry; and because it is an exploitative business, it becomes the focus for our ambivalence towards twentieth-century capitalism: our desire for its fruits warring with our concern for the workers it exploits. On a personal level we have to reconcile our passion for fashion with our guilt at participating in what we perceive as its triviality.

## The Nature of the Relationship

It is apparent that both body image and clothing operate within the same psychological framework, and that this is related to self-awareness. This awareness is largely unconscious, and therefore so is its communication. Communication of the self, it must be remembered, is both internal, concerned with self-understanding, and external, related to our interaction with others. The social psychological processes of identification and differentiation, clearly, are relevant here. As social persons, we need to identify ourselves within a group; as psychological individuals, we need to establish our separate, unique identity. These processes, born of conflict, evoke an individual ambivalence that reflects the cultural ambivalence of society.

If body and clothing operate on the same plane, to address the same issues, it does not necessarily follow that they work together to achieve the same end. The parallels between them are notable, but this does not of itself establish an interrelationship. Nevertheless, their congruence does suggest that probability. *Fashion acts on both the body and clothing choice, and it is possible that, in addressing the conflicts and ambiguities of self-awareness, fashion acts as intermediary between the two.*

Within this context there are two factors that appear to have relevance. Firstly, the concept of the ideal seems to provide a common focus for manipulation of both body and clothing through the medium of fashion. Secondly, the concept of body boundary could provide a point of interaction for ambivalence towards the self, the body and fashion. Since both of these concepts apparently have a part to play in any possible relationship, it is worth considering them in some detail.

### The Concept of the Ideal Body
The concept of the ideal body may be viewed in two ways: the ideal body that we aspire to, or the platonic ideal—that is, the idea of the body as opposed to the actual *body in itself*. In platonic terms, the ideal body is the body that we know; the body in itself we can never know. The platonic ideal is the image that we have created, and may be compared to Lacan's (1977) representation of a body, or Radley's (1998) stylized body. This

is the body of embodiment, and should be contrasted with the object-body. Both are related to the cultural ideal: the object-body is compared with, and assessed in relation to, the cultural ideal; the embodied body is constructed within its framework. Both, in their own way, may be unrealistic: the object-body because it cannot achieve the perfection of the cultural ideal; the embodied body because it is created from a chimera. If this view of the body were correct, then we might expect to find a body image that is both better and worse than the reality—a paradox that could explain why people sometimes choose clothes that apparently do not suit them. Contemporaries, for example, often commented on the unattractiveness of Queen Victoria's crinolines, which, with a diameter approaching six feet, did not sit well on her four-feet-ten-inches height.

Our present-day obsession with the body has been related to the postmodern emphasis on the visual image, and the negative view of the body that results in extreme reactions, such as anorexia nervosa, is blamed on our media bombardment with images of the cultural ideal. However, while it is true to say that we are influenced by the current ideal, this is not just a modern phenomenon. The nature of the ideal may have changed, but individuals have always aspired to whatever the particular ideal of their time has happened to be. We are perhaps more aware of its power at the moment because of the feminist critique of its effect on women.

At different times throughout history, all kinds of body types have represented the ideal: at various times it has been large, small, mature, boyish, etc. The only constant has been height for men: short has never been considered attractive. Because we always see the ideal of our own time as beautiful, we tend to believe that there is a universal standard of beauty, and that, in times past, this was undermined by the fashions of the day. This has been the view of critics of fashion such as Barthes (1983) and Baudrillard (1981). However, bodies have fashions too, and the fashionable body of any era becomes the ideal. It emerges out of the ideas and developments of the time. For example, the *Empire Look,* fashionable at the turn of the nineteenth century, reflected the resurgence of interest in all things classical, and in particular in classical statuary. The draped muslin dresses of the women were designed to emulate the drapery of female statues, and the tight clothes of the men were meant to suggest the naked bodies of male statues. At about the same time the development of steel eyelets enabled the manufacture of more efficient corsets, facilitating the creation of the slim and youthful ideal body of the time.

In the late twentieth century, the ideal has become increasingly thin. This is apparent from the increase in the number of thin females seen on television and film (Silverstein *et al.* 1986), and the trend in the media towards thinner female figures (Garner *et al.* 1980). This trend has been reflected in the steady decline in average weights over the same period (Kaiser 1997); yet it seems that the majority of women still consider themselves overweight compared with the ideal (L. L. Davis 1985). It is tempting to think of this ideal as part of the male objectification of women, but Fallon and Rozin (1985) found that women's ideal is actually thinner than that which they know men find attractive.

The ideal body appears to be a reflection of the unconscious concerns of its time. It is disseminated through images. In the past this has been through the portraits of the time; in the late twentieth century images have proliferated through films, television and fashion magazines. These images are of nude bodies; but, as Berger (1972) has argued, there is a difference between nude, the image of an object-body, and naked, which is the absence of clothes. In art and other representations, the unclothed nude represents the ideal body of its time; but it is created from a clothed ideal. Anne Hollander (1978) describes these nudes as wearing the "ghosts of absent clothes." The images of the ideal are never realistic; Ingres, for example, whose *Grande Odalisque* had a bottom entirely out of proportion with the rest of her body, may be compared with present-day photographers, who airbrush out any extra flesh. It is not surprising, therefore, that we find the less than ideal unacceptable. Flügel (1930), for example, advocated nudism as a means of overcoming the modesty/ eroticism conflict; but he believed that only beautiful bodies, contrived by means of eugenics, should be seen.

Our perception is primarily visual, and our compulsion to create visual images is therefore predictable. We have all experienced this compulsion, as described by Barthes (1984: 10–11), in front of a camera lens: ". . . once I feel myself observed by the lens, everything changes: I constitute myself in the process of 'posing', I instantaneously make another body for myself, I transform myself in advance into an image." In our self-representation, we attempt to make an image of ourselves that corresponds to our sense of the ideal, both in the cultural and the platonic meanings of the word. We strive to make this image real, to transform the real body into the image of the ideal; and we will go to any lengths to achieve this. We are horrified by the cosmetics of earlier times, made of white lead and mercury, which stripped layers of skin away from the wearer, who risked death in order to achieve the white skin admired at the time. Their modern counterparts apply creams containing the chemical rhetinol, which strips the top layers of skin away, in order to achieve the youthful looks that our era admires, and risk death by making their skins over-sensitive to the sun.

Our attempts to transform the body into the ideal body are likely to end in dissatisfaction, because we are attempting to achieve the unachievable. The real body cannot resemble the ideal body, since this is artificially created with imaginary clothes. We must therefore use real clothes in order to create a similar image. Clothes may be said to become the body we wish to present, and fashion allows us to present the current ideal.

## The Role of Body Boundary

The body is more than a biological organism; it is an aspect of the psyche, and Wilson (1985) has suggested that it should also be viewed as a cultural artefact. Body awareness is inseparable from self-awareness; indeed, it represents the frontier of self-cognition. Our sense of self as separate from non-self begins at the edges of the body. This awareness is unconscious, and is described by the hypothetical construct of body boundary.

According to Piaget (1973), self-cognition begins with the infant's grasp of what he called the *object concept*; part of that process is the child's awareness of her own body as a separate object. As the child gains control over her body she begins a process of separating self from non-self; out of this develops the understanding that there are other separate objects in her world, that they have an existence that is independent from hers, and that part of their separateness is a different view of the world. This process provides the foundation for the logical thinking that, Piaget believes, characterizes adult thinking. It is a process of psychological development; but it is rooted in the physical sense of self. The physical aspect becomes even more apparent when we consider criticisms of Piaget's work. Hughes, for example, demonstrated the ability to *decenter* at an earlier age than Piaget (1973) claimed; he accomplished this by means of a three-dimensional model that allowed the child to move dolls physically to different locations, and thus to different perspectives. Implicit in this theory is the idea that, with the development of abstract thinking, the need for a physical perspective is discarded. However, some critics of Piaget have suggested that many adults never reach this higher level of thinking, and the sight of someone turning a map upside down in order to find a route is one example of the way in which we cling to the concrete. Perhaps Bruner's (1966) suggestion that we retain those earlier perspectives, while developing what he calls *symbolic* thinking, is nearer the truth.

The fact that we retain this physicality lends weight to the concept of body boundary as a psychological phenomenon that delineates our psychological sense of self, and is instrumental in our social interactions. It must necessarily be an ambiguous boundary, and, for individual and cultural reasons, individuals differ in the degree of definition they experience. Its relation to clothing has been noted (Fisher 1986), and clothing appears to take on the same quality of ambiguity.

Clothing marks an unclear boundary ambiguously . . .

If the body with its open orifices is itself dangerously ambiguous, then dress, which is an extension of the body yet not quite part of it, not only links that body to the social world, but also more clearly separates the two. Dress is the frontier between the self and the not-self (Wilson 1985:2–3).

Clothing has two faces: one is turned inward, and emphasizes the body's threshold; the other is turned outward and, as Wilson suggests, links the self to others with a common basis for recognition. The fact that it is unconscious makes it all the more powerful. The functions of clothing are multifarious, and each operates according to these two aspects. Table 3 summarizes these operations. It is immediately apparent from this that the complexity and ambiguity of clothing, to a great extent, stems from its boundary role: a role that is inextricably enmeshed in that of the body. The two, it seems, operate together to delineate the self. The ambiguity of body-clothing in this regard is exemplified by the sight of clothing unworn. There is something unsettling about this, particularly about clothes that have been discarded. Wilson (1985) compares it to a snake's skin that has been sloughed off, and many writers have employed the analogy of a corpse (for example, Cavallaro and Warwick 1998). Indeed, Cocteau (1987) speaks of *the soul of a dress [being] the body.*

**Table 3** The Internal and External Aspects of Clothing's Boundary Role

| Inward Aspect | Outward Aspect |
| --- | --- |
| defines the self | de-individualizes the self |
| conceals the self | reveals the self |
| controls the body | creates the ideal body |
| structures the body | makes the body amorphous |
| symbolic of internal states | projection of ideal |
| barrier to social interaction | facilitates social interaction |

Fashion feeds off this ambiguity. The exploration of the boundary, the notion of what is body and what clothing, fuels many of fashion's wilder flights of fancy. The attraction of the panniers of the eighteenth century, and the bustle of the nineteenth, began with the eroticism of the relevant parts of the body, but ended in hugely exaggerated artifacts that could not realistically be mistaken for the real thing. In playing with the boundary, fashion appears to be focusing on its internal/external aspects. This may be because fashion's function is to overlay the real body with the ideal. The designs of Vivienne Westwood, for example, which appear to reveal the body, are in fact carefully constructed to create what for her is the ideal of an hourglass figure; the real body is artfully concealed.

The reveal/conceal aspect is a distinctive theme in fashion. Westwood's cut, Hervé Leger's bandage-like stitching, St Laurent's draping and use of transparent fabric, are all examples of devices that apparently reveal but in reality conceal. Conversely, devices that seem to conceal may be used to reveal. The designs of Shirin Guild are based on the layered clothing traditional to her native Afghanistan. At first sight, the clothes appear loose and formless; but the impression they create of the wearer is of the body underneath. Similarly, the recent use of masks by designers such as Alexander McQueen (1998) highlights the *conceal to reveal* aspect that Barthes (1984), speaking of dark glasses, describes thus: "The hiding must be seen: I want you to know that I am hiding something from you."

In all of these examples, however, what is revealed is not any objective reality, but rather what the designer, or perhaps the wearer, wishes to reveal. When John Rocha showed balaclavas (Spring, 1999) in his collection, it was the glamor of anonymity that was revealed through their association with secret men of violence. The balaclava, recently growing in popularity with fashion designers, is particularly relevant in this context, since it epitomizes the internal/external ambiguity of clothing. Physically, it follows the contours of the face, in the same way that a death mask does; yet simultaneously it protects the wearer from exposure. It both defines and de-individualizes; structures and makes amorphous; conceals and reveals.

The intimate relationship between clothing and body boundary, and the ambiguity they express, seems to be implicit in fashion. The fact that body boundary is an essential aspect of self-awareness suggests that the link between fashion and self may well occur here; and that fashion's role is to address issues of ambivalence sited on the body.

## Conclusion

Fashion's relation to the body appears to be rooted in the ambivalence of both. This ambivalence derives from complex sources of conflict both within the individual and in society. While it is difficult to disentangle the sources of ambivalence, it is nevertheless possible to identify factors inherent in its development, and the following points can be made.

- The communication of the self through the interaction of body and clothing occurs as a result of the juxtaposition of various body/clothing elements. Together these elements create a complex and ambiguous message.
- The body is experienced as part of the process of *selfing*, and is also an outward expression of that self. Fashion, in addressing the ambiguities resulting from internal conflict, communicates both aspects of the self.
- The presentation of the self through body and clothing is subject to the opposing social-psychological drives of identification and differentiation. The ambivalence engendered by their conflict drives fashion change.
- Ambivalence, both within the individual, and in the individual's interaction with society, appears to be central to the body-clothing-fashion experience.

- In clothing the body, the individual attempts to create the ideal body: an ideal that both expresses the embodied self and aspires to the cultural ideal. Fashion operates at the level of the latter.
- Body and clothing appear to operate together to delineate the self; in so doing they form an interface that is manipulated by fashion, possibly to achieve the ideal.

Much of our ambivalence appears to focus on this body–clothing interface. The body, as both experience and expression of the self, delineates the ambivalence that we experience from within and are subject to from without. At first sight, clothing appears as an avocation of this ambivalence; but body and clothing are so intertwined that they cannot, in this context, be seen as independent. Fashion alludes to the cultural ideal, and manipulates the body–clothing interface in order to achieve it. Yet both fashion and the ideal are themselves sources of ambivalence. Because it is superficial, we relegate fashion to the level of the trivial; at the same time, however, we are unable to resist what Quentin Bell (1976) has described as its "tyranny." Similarly, we aspire to the ideal, while at the same time resenting its power. Ambivalence, then, lies at the center of the interaction between body and fashion. The ambiguity of the body–clothing interface suggests that this may be the source of their relationship, and as such, it is worthy of further investigation.

## References

Adams, G. R. and P. Crane. 1980. "An Assumption of Parents' and Teachers' Expectations of Preschool Children's Social Preference for Attractive or Unattractive Children or Adults." *Child Development*, 51: 224–31.

Adorno, T. 1967. *Prisms*. Cambridge, MA: MIT Press.

Asch, S. E. 1956. "Studies of Independence and Submission to Group Pressure: 1 A Minority of One Against a Unanimous Majority." *Psychological Monographs*, 70: (9) (Whole No. 416).

Baerveldt, C, and P. Voestermans. 1998. "The Body as a Selfing Device." In Henderikus J. Stam (ed.), *The Body and Psychology*. London: Sage Publications.

Bandura, A. 1977. *Social Learning Theory*. Englewood Cliffs, NJ: Prentice Hall.

Barthes, R. 1983. *The Fashion System*, trans. M. Ward and R. Howard. London: Jonathan Cape.

——. 1984. *Camera Lucida*. London: Fontana.

Baudrillard, J. 1975. *The Mirror of Production*. St. Louis: Telos Press.

——. 1981. *For a Critique of the Political Economy of the Sign*. St. Louis: Telos Press.

Bell, Q. 1976. *On Human Finery*. London: Hogarth Press.

Berger, J. 1972. *Ways of Seeing*. London: British Broadcasting Corporation.

Berscheid, E. and E. Walster. 1974. "Physical Attractiveness." In L. Berkowitz (ed.) *Advances in Experimental Social Psychology*. New York: Academic Press.

Berscheid, E., K. Dion, E. Walster, and G. W. Walster. 1971. "Physical Attractiveness and Dating Choice: A Test of the Matching Hypothesis." *Journal of Experimental Social Psychology*. 7: 173–80.

Blos, P. 1967. "The Second Individuation Process of Adolescence." *Psychoanalytic Study of the Child*, 22: 162–86.

Blumer, H. 1969. "Fashion: From Class Differentiation to Collective Selection." *Sociological Quarterly*, 10: 275–91.

Bruner, J. S. 1966. *Towards a Theory of Instruction*. Cambridge, MA: Harvard University Press.

Buckley, H. M. 1983. "Attraction Toward a Stranger as a Linear Function of Similarity in Dress." *Home Economics Research Journal*, 12: 25–33.

Cavallaro, D. and A. Warwick. 1998. *Fashioning the Frame: Boundaries, Dress and Body*. Oxford: Berg.

Chang, Jung. 1991. *Wild Swans*. London: HarperCollins.

Cocteau, Jean. 1987. *Past Tense, Volume 1: Diaries* (English translation). London: Harcourt Brace.

Creekmore, A. M. 1980. "Clothing and Personal Attractiveness of Adolescents Related to Conformity to Clothing Mode, Peer Acceptance and Leadership Potential." *Home Economics Research Journal*, 8: (3): 203–15.

Davis, F. 1985. "Clothing and Fashion as Communication." In M. R. Solomon (ed.) *The Psychology of Fashion*, pp. 15–27. Lexington: Lexington Books.

— —. 1992. *Fashion, Culture and Identity*. Chicago: University of Chicago Press.

Davis, L. L. 1985. "Perceived Somatotype, Body-cathexis, and Attitudes Toward Clothing among College Females." *Perceptual and Motor Skills*, 61: 1199–1205.

Dion, K. K., E. Berscheid, and E. Walster. 1972. "What is Beautiful is Good." *Journal of Personality and Social Psychology*, 14: 97–108.

Fallon, A. E. and P. Rozin. 1985. "Short Reports: Sex Differences in Perceptions of Desirable Body Shape." *Journal of Abnormal Psychology*, 94: 102–5.

Feldman, R. E. 1972. "Response to Compatriot and Foreigner Who Seek Assistance." In L. Bickman and T. Hencky (eds), *Beyond the Laboratory: Field Research in Social Psychology*. New York: McGraw Hill.

Festinger, L. 1957. *A Theory of Cognitive Dissonance*. New York: Harper and Row.

Fisher, S. 1986. *Development and Structure of the Body Image*. Hillsdale: Lawrence Erlbaum.

Flügel, J. C. 1930. *The Psychology of Clothes*. London: Hogarth Press.

Frederickson, B. L., T.-A. Roberts, S. M. Noll, D. M. Quinn, and J. M. Twenge. 1998. "That Swimsuit Becomes You: Sex Differences in Self-objectification, Restrained Eating and Math Performance." *Journal of Personality and Social Psychology*, 75: 269–85.

Freud, S. 1963. *Complete Psychological Works of Sigmund Freud*. London: Chatto & Windus.

Garner, D. M., P. E. Garfinkel, D. Schwartz, and M. Thompson. 1980. "Cultural Expectations on Thinness in Women." *Psychological Reports*, 47: 482–91.

Goffman, E. 1971. *The Presentation of Self in Everyday Life*. Harmondsworth: Penguin.

Greer, Germaine. 1999. *The Whole Woman*. New York: Doubleday.

Gurel, L. M., J. C. Wilbur, and L. Gurel. 1972. "Personality Correlates of Adolescent Clothing Styles." *Journal of Home Economics*, 64: 42–7.

Harman, L. D. 1985. "Acceptable Deviance as Social Control: The Cases of Fashion and Slang." *Deviant Behaviour*, 6: 1–15.

Harré, R. and G. Gillett. 1994. *The Discursive Mind*. London: Sage.

Hebdige, D. 1979. *Subculture: The Meaning of Style*. London: Methuen.

Hollander, Anne. 1978. *Seeing Through Clothes*. New York: Viking.

Irigaray, L. 1985. *This Sex Which Is Not One*. Ithaca, NY: Cornell University Press.

Kaiser, S. B. 1997. *The Social Psychology of Clothing: Symbolic Appearances in Context*, 2nd edition revised. New York: Fairchild.

Kaiser, S. B., C. M. Freeman, and J. L. Chandler. 1993. "Favorite Clothes and Gendered Subjectivities: Multiple Readings." In N. K. Denzin (ed.), *Studies in Symbolic Interaction*, Vol. 15, pp. 27–50. Greenwich, CT: JAI Press Inc.

Kaiser, S. B., R. H. Nagasawa, and S. S. Hutton. 1995. "Construction of an SI Theory of Fashion: Part 1. Ambivalence and Change." *Clothing and Textiles Research Journal*, 13 (3): 172–83.

King, C. W. 1963. "Fashion Adoption: A Rebuttal to the 'Trickle-down' Theory." In S. A. Greyser (ed.), *Toward Scientific Marketing*, pp. 108–25. Chicago: Chicago American Marketing Association.

König, R. 1973. *The Restless Image*. London: George Allen & Unwin.

Lacan, J. 1977. *Ecrits: A Selection*, trans. A Sheridan. London: Tavistock Publications.

Lennon, S. J. and F. G. Miller. 1984–85. "Attire, Physical Appearance, and First Impressions: More is Less." *Clothing and Textiles Research Journal*, 3 (1): 1–8.

Lurie, A. 1992. *The Language of Clothes*, 1st edition revised. London: Bloomsbury Publishing .

McCracken, G. 1988. *Culture and Consumption*. Bloomington, IN: Indiana University Press.

Piaget, J. 1973. *The Child's Conception of the World*. London: Paladin.

Radley, A. 1991. *The Body and Social Psychology.* New York: Springer.
——. 1998. "Displays and Fragments: Embodiment and the Configuration of Social Worlds." In Henderikus J. Stam (ed.), *The Body and Psychology.* London: Sage.
Sheehy, G. 1976. *Passages—Predictable Crises of Adult Life.* New York: Bantam Books.
Sigall, H. and N. Ostrove. 1975. "Beautiful but Dangerous: Effects of Offender Attractiveness and Nature of the Crime on Juridic Judgement." *Journal of Personality and Social Psychology*, 31: 410–14.
Silverstein, B., L. Perdue, B. Peterson, and E. Kelly. 1986. "The Role of the Mass Media in Promoting a Thin Standard of Bodily Attractiveness for Women." *Sex Roles*, 14: 519–32.
Simmel, G. 1904. "Fashion." *International Quarterly*, 10: 130–55.
——. 1991. "The Problem of Style." *Theory, Culture and Society*, 8: 63–71.
Snyder, C. R. and H. L. Fromkin. 1980. *Uniqueness: The Human Pursuit of Difference.* New York: Plenum Press.
Stone, G. P. 1965. "Appearance and the Self." In M. E. Roach and J. B. Eicher (eds), *Dress and Adornment, and the Social Order.* New York: John Wiley & Sons.
Toffler, A. 1980. *The Third Wave.* New York: William Morrow & Co.
Turner, B. S. 1984. *The Body and Society.* New York: Basil Blackwell.
Wilson, E. 1985. *Adorned in Dreams: Fashion and Modernity.* London: Virago.
Woolf, Virginia. 1966. *The New Dress.* In Virginia Woolf, *The Haunted House and Other Stories.* London: Harvest Books.

*Fashion Theory*, Volume 4, Issue 3, pp.323–348
Reprints available directly from the Publishers.
Photocopying permitted by licence only.
© 2000 Berg. Printed in the United Kingdom.

# Fashion and the Fleshy Body: Dress as Embodied Practice

**Joanne Entwistle**

Joanne Entwistle is Lecturer in Sociology at the University of Essex. She is author of *The Fashioned Body: Fashion, Dress and Modern Social Theory* (Polity) and is currently researching workers in the fashion industry.

## Introduction

"There is an obvious and prominent fact about human beings," notes Turner (1985: 1) at the start of *The Body and Society,* "they have bodies and they are bodies." However, what Turner omits in his analysis is another obvious and prominent fact: that human bodies are *dressed* bodies. Dress is a basic fact of social life and this, according to anthropologists, is true of all human cultures that we know about: all cultures "dress" the body in some way, be it through clothing, tattooing, cosmetics or other forms of body painting (Polhemus 1988; Polhemus and Proctor 1978). Conventions of dress transform flesh into something recognizable and meaningful to a culture and are also the means by which bodies are made "decent," appropriate and acceptable within specific contexts. Dress does not merely serve to protect our modesty and does not simply *reflect* a natural body or, for that matter, a given identity; it *embellishes* the body, the materials commonly used adding a whole array of meanings to the body that would otherwise not be there. While the social world normally demands that we appear dressed, what constitutes "dress" varies from culture to culture and also within a culture, since what is considered appropriate dress will vary according to the situation or occasion. The few mere scraps of fabric that make up a bikini are enough to ensure that the female body is "decent" on beaches in the West, but would be entirely inappropriate in the boardroom. Bodies that do not conform, bodies that flout the conventions of their culture and go without the appropriate clothes are subversive of the most basic social codes, and risk exclusion, scorn or ridicule. The "streaker" who strips off and runs across a cricket pitch or soccer stadium draws attention to these conventions in the act of breaking them: indeed, female streaking is defined as a "public order offence," while the "flasher," by comparison, can be punished for "indecent exposure." As these examples illustrate, dress is fundamental to microsocial order, and the exposure of naked flesh is, potentially at least, disruptive of that order. Indeed, nakedness, in those exceptional situations where it is deemed appropriate, has to be carefully managed (nude bathing in the UK and other Western countries is regulated and restricted; doctors must pay close attention to ethical codes of practice, and so on). So fundamental is dress to the social presentation of the body and the social order that it governs even our ways of seeing the naked body. According to Hollander (1993), dress is crucial to our understanding of the body to the extent that our ways of seeing and representing the naked body are dominated by conventions of dress. As she (1993: xiii) argues, "art proves that nakedness is not universally experienced and perceived any more than clothes are. At any time, the unadorned self has more kinship with its own usual *dressed* aspect than it has with any undressed human selves in other times and other places." Hollander points to the ways in which depictions of the nude in art and sculpture correspond to the dominant fashions of the day. Thus the nude is never naked, but "clothed" by contemporary conventions of dress. Naked or semi-naked bodies that break with cultural conventions, especially conventions of gender, are potentially subversive and are treated with horror or derision. Competitive female body-builders, such as those documented in the 1984 semi-documentary film *Pumping Iron II: The Women*, are frequently seen as "monstrous" (Kuhn 1988: 16; see also Schulze 1990 and St Martin and Gavey 1996).

However, while dress cannot be understood without reference to the body and while the body has always and everywhere to be dressed, there has been a surprising lack of concrete analysis of the relationship between them. In this article, I want to flesh out a study of the dressed body that attempts to bridge the gap that exists between theories of the body, which often overlook dress, and theories of fashion and dress, which too frequently leave out the body. I want to suggest some of the connections that can be made between the various theorists in these related areas, suggesting how one might make a study of the dressed body. In doing so, I sketch out a theoretical framework that takes as its starting-point the idea that dress is an embodied practice, a *situated bodily practice* that is embedded within the social world and fundamental to microsocial order (Entwistle 2000a). While emphasizing the social nature of dress, this framework also asserts the idea that individuals/subjects are active in their engagement with the social and that dress is thus actively produced through routine practices directed towards the body. In order to capture this sense of dress as both socially structured and embodied and practical, I shall draw on a wide range of theoretical resources.

The main discussion will focus on the uses and limitations of both the structuralist and post-structuralist approaches, since these have been influential in recent years in the sociological study of the body. In particular, the work of Mary Douglas (1973, 1984), Marcel Mauss (1973) and Michel Foucault (1977, 1986) offers fruitful insights into the way in which the body is rendered meaningful by culture. However, such approaches are limited when it comes to acknowledging the "fleshy" body and its experiential dimensions. They also neglect to account for how structures and rules result in actual embodied practices, sometimes with the effect of reducing individuals to puppet-like actors. In contrast, the phenomenology of Maurice Merleau-Ponty (1976, 1981), which begins with the idea of the body as the "existential ground of culture" (Csordas 1993), is suggestive of the ways in which dress can be understood as an *embodied practice*. These theoretical traditions may seem at odds with one another; and indeed, according to Crossley (1996), they have been considered incommensurable by some. However, as he argues, they offer different and complementary insights into the body and embodiment in society. Following Crossley (1995a, 1995b, 1996) and also Csordas (1993, 1996), I shall argue that an account of dress as a situated bodily practice can draw on the insights of these two different traditions, structuralism and phenomenology, and indeed must do so. Dress as both a social and a personal experience is a discursive and practical phenomenon. A study of the dressed body thus requires understanding of the socially processed body that discourses on dress and fashion shape, as well as of the experiential dimensions of embodiment wherein dress is translated into actual bodily presentation. In addition to these two paradigms, Goffman (1971, 1972) and Bourdieu (1984, 1989, 1994) are particularly useful in that they both bridge the gap between these traditions and acknowledge how social structures are reproduced at the level of bodily practices.

## Ad-dressing the Literature

If nakedness is unruly and disruptive, this would seem to indicate that dress is a fundamental aspect of microsocial order. When we dress we do so to make our bodies acceptable to a social situation. Given this issue of social order, it seems strange to find little discussion of dress within sociology and other disciplines that have been concerned with this on both a macro and a micro level (for example in the work of Parsons and Goffman). This would seem strange given that the force of pressure on the body to conform has a moral imperative to it as well. Dressed inappropriately we are uncomfortable; we feel ourselves open to social condemnation. According to Bell (1976), wearing the right clothes is so very important that even people not interested in their appearance will dress well enough to avoid social censure. In this sense, he argues, we enter into the realm of feelings "prudential, ethical and aesthetic, and the workings of what one might call sartorial conscience" (1976: 18–19). Classical social theory failed to acknowledge the significance of dress, largely because it neglected the body and the things that bodies do (Turner 1985). The emergence of a sociology of the body in the last twenty years would seem an obvious place to look for literature on dress and fashion; but, as with mainstream sociology, it too has also tended not to examine dress (as noted above, Turner does not discuss dress in his account of bodily order). Moreover, the literature on fashion and dress, coming out of history, cultural studies and other fields, has paid little attention to the body, focusing instead on the communicative aspects of adornment (adopting a rather abstract and disembodied linguistic model from Saussure) and examining the spectacular, creative and expressive aspects of dress rather than the mundane and routine part it plays in reproducing social order (Barthes 1985; Hebdige 1979; Lurie 1981; Polhemus 1994).

Between these bodies of literature, between the theorists of the classical tradition and those theorists of the body who tend to overlook dress, and those theorists of fashion and dress who have focused rather too much attention on the articles of clothing, the *dressed body* as a discursive and phenomenological field vanishes. Either the body is thought to be self-evidently dressed (and therefore beyond discussion) or the clothes are assumed to stand up on their own, possibly even speaking for themselves without the aid of the body. And yet the importance of the body to dress is such that encounters with dress divorced from the body are strangely alienating. Wilson (1985) grasps this when she describes the unease one feels in the presence of mannequins in a costume museum. The eeriness of the encounter comes from the "dusty silence" and stillness of the costumes, and from a sense that the museum is "haunted" by the spirits of the living, breathing humans whose bodies these gowns once adorned. Our experience of the costume museum, along with our sadness when confronted with the clothes of dead relatives, points to the ways in which we "normally" experience dress as alive and "fleshy": once removed from the body, dress lacks fullness and seems strange, almost alien, and all the more poignant to us if we can remember the person who once breathed life into the fabric. The body and dress operate dialectically: dress works on the body, imbuing it with social meaning, while the body is a dynamic field that gives life and fullness to dress (Entwistle and Wilson 1998). Thus the dressed body is a fleshy, phenomenological entity that is so much a part of our experience of the social world, so thoroughly embedded within the micro-dynamics of social order, as to be entirely taken for granted. With a growing literature emerging on fashion, dress, the body, embodiment, and performativity, it seems almost a cliché to insist that fashion and dress operate on the body and that, by implication, the body and dress are now a crucial arenas for the performance and articulation of identities. And yet the precise relationship of the body to dress and dress to the body remains unclear and under-theorized. In the discussion that follows, I want to suggest the theoretical resources that can be brought to bear on the analysis of the dressed body as situated practice.

## Situating the Dressed Body in the Social World

Dress lies at the margins of the body and marks the boundary between self and other, individual and society. This boundary is intimate and personal, since our dress forms the visible envelope of the self and, as Davis puts it, comes "to serve as a kind of visual metaphor for identity"; it is also social, since our dress is structured by social forces and subject to social and moral pressures. If, as Mary Douglas (1973, 1984) has so forcefully demonstrated, the boundaries of the body are dangerous, it is therefore no surprise that clothing and other forms of adornment, which operate at these "leaky" margins, are subject to social regulation and moral pronouncements. It is no surprise either to find individuals concerned with what to hang at these margins. Douglas articulates this relationship between the individual body and the social forces pressing on it, arguing that there are "two bodies": the physical body and the social body. She summarizes (1973: 93) the relationship between them in *Natural Symbols*: "the social body constrains the way the physical body is perceived. The physical experience of the body, always modified by the social categories through which it is known, sustains a particular view of society. There is a continual exchange of meanings between the two kinds of bodily experience so that each reinforces the categories of the other." According to Douglas, "the body is capable of furnishing a natural system of symbols" (1973: 12). This means that the body is a highly restricted medium of expression, since it is heavily mediated by culture and expresses the social pressure brought to bear on it. Indeed, the body becomes a symbol of its cultural location. She gives the example of laughter, arguing that the social situation determines the degree to which the body can laugh: the looser the social constraints, the more free the body is to laugh out loud. In this way, the body and its functions and boundaries symbolically articulate the concerns of the particular group in which it is found. Her analysis (1973) of shaggy and smooth hair also illustrates this relationship between the body and the situation. Shaggy hair, once a symbol of rebellion, can be found among those professionals who are in a position to critique society, in particular, academics and artists. Smooth hair, however, is likely to be found among those who conform, such as lawyers and bankers. This analysis can of course be extended to the analysis of dress and adornment. The dressed body is always situated within a particular context, which often sets constraints as to what is and what is not appropriate to wear. The degree to which the dressed body can express itself can therefore be symbolic of this location: for example, the more formal and conservative the occupation, the more constraints set around the body and thus on dress. Therefore traditional or conservative occupations are likely to have stricter codes of dress and necessitate the wearing of a suit, while more "creative" professions will set few restrictions on the body and dress.

Mauss (1973) has likewise discussed the way in which the physical body is shaped by culture when he elaborates on mundane "techniques of the body," and these have some potential for understanding the situated nature of the dressed body. The techniques he outlines are not "natural," but the product of particular ways of being in the body that are embedded within culture and his examples also point to the ways in which these are gendered. Ways of walking, moving, making a fist, and so on, are different for men and women because, in the making of "masculine" and "feminine," culture inscribes the bodies of men and women with different physical capacities. Mauss's "techniques of the body" have obvious application to dress and the way in which dress modifies the body, embellishing it and inflecting it with meanings that, in the first instance, are gendered. Although he says little about dress, he does note how women learn to walk in high heels that would be difficult and uncomfortable for men, who are generally unaccustomed to such shoes. Illustrative of this particular technique in her exaggeration of it is Marilyn Monroe's sashaying gait in *Some Like It Hot*, which was apparently the product of high heels cut diagonally at each side. These lop-sided shoes enabled her to generate the wiggle that constituted part of her performance as the sexually provocative Sugar Cane.

Although they don't acknowledge Mauss's work, Haug *et. al.* (1987) provide ample evidence of the ways in which femininity is reproduced through various techniques, bodily and sartorial. They argue that the female body and its ways of being and adorning are the product of particular discourses of the body that are inherently gendered. These discourses are explored through the work of Foucault; and I want to suggest some of the ways in which his concept of discourse, with its emphasis on the body, could be utilized for analysis of the situated nature of the body.

In *Discipline and Punish* Foucault (1977) argues that bodily practices are part of the capillary like operations of power which work to render bodies docile, obedient. While feminists such as McNay (1992) and Diamond and Quinby (1988) argue that Foucault ignores the issue of gender, they also point out that his theoretical concepts can provide feminists with a framework for understanding the ways in which the body is acted on by power/knowledge. Indeed, Foucault's notion of discourse can enable the analysis of fashion as a discursive domain that sets significant parameters around the body and its presentation. Fashion (defined here as a system of continually changing styles), which sets out an array of competing discourses on image and is the dominant system governing dress in the West, has been linked to the operations of power, initially marking out class divisions, but more recently playing a crucial role in policing the boundaries of sexual difference.

Although utilized by Wilson (1992), Foucault's work on the body has not been usefully employed in the analysis of fashion as a textual site for the construction of the body, although it would seem that it would have some application. Fashion, particularly as it is laid out in the fashion magazine, is "obsessed with gender" (Wilson 1985: 117), and constantly shifts the boundary between the genders. This preoccupation with gender starts with babies and is played out through the life cycle, so that styles of dress at significant moments are very clearly gendered (weddings and other formal occasions are the most obvious examples). Such styles enable the repetitious production of gender, even when gender appears to break down, as with androgynous fashion, and are aided in part by the repetition of gendered styles of bodily posture routinely reproduced in fashion magazines. While these styles of being reproduce gender as a body style, they are also open to subversion through exaggeration and parody, as Butler (1990, 1993) has forcefully suggested, although some of the most exaggerated performances, such as drag, could be said to reinforce rather than undermine conventions of gender (Gamman and Makinen 1994).

In addition, Foucault's insights into the ways in which bodies are subject to power and discursively constituted can be utilized to show how institutional and discursive practices of dress act upon the body, marking it and rendering it meaningful and productive. For example, styles of dress are regularly employed in the workplace as part of institutional and corporate strategies of management. This is explored by Freeman (1993), who draws on Foucault's notion of power, particularly his idea about the panopticon, to consider how dress is used in one particular context, a data-processing corporation, *Data Air*, as a strategy of corporate discipline and control over the female workforce. In this corporation a strict dress code insisted that the predominantly female workers dress "smartly" in order to project a "modern" and "professional" image of the corporation. If their dress does not meet this standard they are subjected to disciplinary procedures by their managers, and may even be sent home to change their clothes. The enforcement of this dress code was facilitated by the open-plan office, which kept the women under constant surveillance by the gaze of managers.

Such practices are familiar to many offices although the mechanisms for enforcing dress codes vary enormously. Particular discourses of dress such as "smart" or "professional" dress, and particular strategies of dress such as the imposition of uniforms and dress codes at work, are utilized by corporations to exercise control over the bodies of the workers within. This is true of men's dress for work as much as it is of women's. The male suit, perhaps the most formally coded dress for men today, exerts itself with considerable force over the bodies of men in a wide range of occupational settings, while looser codes of bodily presentation are often set over the bodies of "professionals," who, rather than being told what to wear, are expected to have internalized the codes of the profession. For example, the discourse of power dressing, which I have analyzed elsewhere (Entwistle 1997, 2000a, 2000b), sets out clear codes of dressing for success; but its adoption by professionals is largely dependent upon their having internalized a particular notion of themselves as "enterprising" subjects. The discourse on power dressing called upon career women to think about and act upon their bodies in particular ways as part of an overall "project of the self" (Giddens 1991) in order to maximize one's chances of career success. The rules of such dressing as delineated in dress manuals and magazine articles set out a strategy of dressing for work that relies on technical knowledge of dress and its "effects" (the term "wardrobe engineering," devised by the most famous exponent of power dressing John T. Molloy (1980), captures this technical and instrumental concern).

As I have demonstrated, Foucault's framework is quite useful for analyzing the discursive aspects of dress. In particular, his notion of discourse is a good starting-point for analyzing the relations between discourses on dress and gender as they are constituted in fashion texts and organizational strategies of management and are suggestive of particular forms of discipline of the body. However, there are problems with Foucault's notion of discourse as well as problems stemming from his conceptualization of the body and of power, in particular his failure to acknowledge embodiment and agency. These problems stem from Foucault's post-structuralist philosophy, and these I now want to summarize in order to suggest how his theoretical perspective, while useful in some respects, particularly for textual analysis, is problematic for a study of dress as a situated bodily practice. In other words, his theoretical concepts do not stretch to the analysis of dress as an embodied practice.

Foucault's account of the socially processed body provides for analysis of the way in which the body is talked about and acted on; but it does not provide an account of dress as it is lived, experienced and embodied by individuals. For example, the existence of the corset in the nineteenth century and the discourses about the supposed morality of wearing one (the terms "loose" and "straitlaced" used to describe a woman refer to the wearing of a corset, and illustrate, if metaphorically, the link between this article of clothing and morality) tell us little or nothing about how Victorian women experienced the corset, how tightly they chose to lace it, and what bodily sensations it produced. However, it would seem that by investing importance in the body, dress opens up the potential for women to use this for their own purposes and experience pleasures that are perhaps the "reverse" of dominant ones. However, as Ramazanoglu (1993) argues, while the notion of reverse discourse is potentially very useful to feminists, it is not developed fully in Foucault's analysis. So while the corset is seen by some feminists (Roberts 1977) as a garment setting out to discipline the female body and make her "docile" and subservient, an "exquisite slave," Kunzle (1982) has argued in relation to female tight-lacers that these women were not passive or masochistic victims of patriarchy, but socially and sexually assertive. Kunzle's suggestion is that women more than men have used their sexuality to climb the social ladder, and that tight-lacers experienced sexual pleasures from the tightly laced corset that went against the dominant norm of the Victorian woman as asexual. If his analysis is accepted, these particular Victorian women could be said to illustrate the ways in which power, once invested in the female body, results in "the responding claims and affirmations, those of one's own body against power . . . of pleasure against the moral norms of sexuality, marriage, decency . . ." (Foucault 1980: 56). In other words, illustrative of "reverse discourse."

However, this issue lies dormant in Foucault's own analysis, partly because Foucault's particular form of post-structuralism is not sensitive to *practice*. Instead it *presumes* effects, at the level of individual practice, from the existence of discourse alone. He thus "reads" texts *as if* they were practice rather than a possible structuring influence on practice that might or might not be implemented. In assuming that discourse automatically has social effects, Foucault's method, as Turner (1985: 175) notes, "reduce(s) the individual agent to a socialized parrot which must speak/perform in a determinate manner in accordance with the rules of language." In failing to produce any account of how discourses get taken up in practices, Foucault also fails to give an adequate explanation as to how resistance to discourse is possible.

Moreover, his analysis lacks sensitivity to the body as the environment of the self and tends to assume a notion of the "passive body," thereby failing to explain how individuals may act in an autonomous fashion. If bodies are produced and manipulated by power, then this would seem to contradict Foucault's concern to see power as force relations that are never simply oppressive. Such an account might lead to the discussion of fashion and dress as merely constraining social forces and thus neglect the way individuals can be active in their selective choices from fashion discourse in their everyday experience of dress.

The extreme anti-humanism of Foucault's work, most notably in *Discipline and Punish*, is questioned by McNay (1992) because it does not allow for notions of subjectivity and experience, and she proposes that his later work on "technologies of the self" offers a more useful theoretical framework. However, as she herself later acknowledges (McNay 1999), Foucault's notion of subjectivity as developed in his "technologies of self" is disconnected from his earlier work on the body, and is thus strangely disembodied. In terms of producing an account of embodiment and of agency, McNay suggests that Bourdieu's notions of the *habitus* and *the field* are more productive. If the dressed body is to be understood as always situated in culture and as an embodied activity located within specific temporal and spatial relations, then these concepts from Bourdieu offer much potential. I shall discuss Bourdieu's work in more detail below.

Further problems arise from Foucault's rather ambivalent notion of the body: on the one hand, his bio-politics would appear to construct the body as a concrete, material entity, manipulated by institutions and practices; on the other hand, his focus on discourse seems to produce a notion of the body that has no materiality outside the representation. Such a vacillation is problematic, since the question of what constitutes a body is one that cannot be avoided—does the body have a materiality outside language and representation? The body cannot be at one and the same time both a material object outside of language and a solely linguistic construction. This refusal to develop an ontology of the body fits with Foucault's general refusal of all essence, as Turner (1985) notes. However, Terence Turner (1996: 37) goes so far as to suggest that Foucault's body is more contradictory and problematic in terms of his own claim to critique essences: it is "a featureless *tabula rasa* awaiting the animating disciplines of discourse . . . an a priori individual unity disarmingly reminiscent of its arch-rival, the transcendental subject." If, as it seems, Foucault errs on the side of the body as a discursive construct this would appear to undermine his aim to produce a "history of bodies" and the investments and operations of power on them. What is most material and most vital about a body if not its flesh and bones? What is power doing if not operating on, controlling or dominating the material body?

However, if the body has its own physical reality outside or beyond discourse, how can we theorize this experience? How can one begin to understand the experience of choosing and wearing clothes that forms so significant a part of our experience of our body/self? With these issues in mind, Csordas (1993, 1996) details the way forward for what he calls a "paradigm of embodiment," which he poses as an alternative to the "paradigm of the body" that characterizes the structuralist approach. This methodological shift "requires that the body be understood as the existential ground of culture—not an object that is 'good to think with' but as a subject that is 'necessary to be'" (1993: 135). The body, in phenomenological terms, is the environment of the self, and therefore something acted upon as part of the experience of selfhood. This is in contrast to the semiotic model, which considers the body as a symbolic and discursive object worked on by culture. Csordas's express aim is therefore to counter-balance the "strong representational bias" of the semiotic/textual paradigm found in works such as that of Douglas (1973, 1979), Foucault (1977) and Derrida (1976). Csordas calls for a shift away from a semiotic/textualist framework to a notion of embodiment and "being in the world" drawn from phenomenology.

He notes how, "of all the formal definitions of culture that have been proposed by anthropology, none have taken seriously the idea that culture is grounded in the human body" (Csordas 1996: 6). Thus the phenomenological concern with embodiment starts from a different premise to structuralist and post-structuralist accounts of the social world, positioning the body as "the existential ground of culture and self" (Csordas 1993). He argues for a study of embodiment that draws on the phenomenology of Merleau-Ponty (1976, 1981) as well as Bourdieu's (1989) "theory of practice." His paradigm of embodiment thus marks a methodological shift away from a concern with texts to a concern with *bodily experience* and *social practice*. According to Csordas, both Merleau-Ponty (1976, 1981) and Bourdieu (1989, 1994) shift the concern away from the body as an inert object to an idea of the body as implicated in everyday perception and practices. A similar distinction is drawn by Crossley (1995a, 1995b, 1996), who argues that the "sociology of the body" is concerned with "what is done to the body," while "carnal sociology" examines "what the body does" (1995b: 43). He, too, identifies this latter tradition with the work of Merleau-Ponty, but looks also to Goffman whose account of microsocial interactions positions the body as the central vehicle of the "self." In the following section, I want to detail the theoretical and methodological assumptions underlying a "paradigm of embodiment," drawing on the work of Merleau-Ponty, and suggest how phenomenology might enable a study of dress as situated practice. I want also to suggest how the work of Bourdieu and Goffman may be applied to the study of the dressed body and how their insights bridge the gap between structuralist and phenomenological concepts. In the work of both, the body is both a socially constituted object, determined by social structures, and yet also the site of social and personal identity.

## Dress and Embodiment

Merleau-Ponty (1976, 1981) places the body at the center of his analysis of perception, arguing that the world comes to us via perceptive awareness, i.e., from the place of our body in the world. Merleau-Ponty stresses the simple fact that the mind is situated in the body and comes to know the world through what he called "corporeal or postural schema": in other words we grasp external space, relationships between objects and our relationship to them through our position in, and movement through, the world. Thus the aim of his work on perception, as he (1976: 3–4) points out in *The Primacy of Perception*, is to "re-establish the roots of the mind in its body and in its world, going against doctrines which treat perception as a simple result of the action of external things on our body as well as against those which insist on the autonomy of consciousness." As a result of his emphasis on perception and experience, subjects are reinstated as temporal and spatial beings. Rather than being "an object in the world" the body forms our "point of view on the world" (1976: 5). In this way, Merleau-Ponty counteracts the tendency in Foucault to see the body as a passive object. According to Merleau-Ponty, we come to understand our relation in the world via the positioning of our body physically and historically in space. "Far from being merely an instrument or object in the world our bodies are what give us our expression in the world" (1976: 5). In other words, our body is not just the place from which we come to experience the world; it is through our bodies that we come to see and be seen in the world. The body forms the envelope of our being in the world, and our selfhood comes from this location in our body and our experience of this. In terms of dress, approaching it from a phenomenological framework means acknowledging the way in which dress works on the body which in turn works on and mediates the experience of self. Eco (1986) captures this very well when he describes wearing jeans that are still too tight after losing some weight. He (1986: 192–4) describes how the jeans feel on his body, how they pinch and how they restrict his movement, how they make him aware of the lower half of his body; indeed, how they come to constitute an "epidermic self-awareness" that he had not felt before:

> As a result, I lived in the knowledge that I had jeans on, whereas normally we live forgetting that we're wearing undershorts or trousers. I lived for my jeans and as a result I assumed an exterior behavior of one who wears jeans. In any case, I assumed a demeanor . . . Not only did the garment impose a demeanor on me; by focusing my attention on demeanor it obliged me to live towards the exterior world.

If, for the most part, we don't experience our jeans (or any other item of clothing for that matter) in this way, then this hints at our "normal" experience of dress and its relationship to the body; namely that it becomes an extension of the body that is like a second skin. Dressed uncomfortably, on the other hand, we may develop the "epidermic self-awareness" Eco refers to since the garment/s impinge upon our experience of the body and make us aware of the "edges," the limits and boundaries of our body. This body/dress awareness is gendered: as Tseëlon (1997: 61) notes, women's sense of self (and self-worth) is frequently a "fragile" one, and dress can either bolster confidence or make one acutely self-conscious and uncomfortable.

Merleau-Ponty's notion of subjectivity is neither essential nor transcendental: the self is located in a body, which in turn is located in time and space. The notion of space was for Merleau-Ponty crucial to the phenomenology of lived experience, since the movement of bodies through space was an important feature of their perception of the world and their relationship to others and objects in the world. This concern with space is apparent in Foucault's work on the institutions of modernity; but while his account of space acknowledges its disciplinary and political dimensions, it lacks any sense of how people experience space. Foucault's analysis looks at space in relation to social order and, ultimately, power: a phenomenological analysis of space, such as that offered by Merleau-Ponty, considers how we grasp external space via our bodily situation or "corporeal or postural schema" (1976: 5). Thus, "our body is not in space like things; it inhabits or haunts space" (1976: 5). For Merleau-Ponty, body/subjects are always subjects in space; but our experience of it comes from our movement around the world and our grasping of objects in that space through perceptual awareness. Space is grasped, actively seized upon by individuals through their embodied encounter with it. Of course, space is a crucial aspect of our experience of the dressed body, since when we get dressed we do so with implicit understanding of the rules and norms of particular social spaces. A formal dinner, a job interview, a shopping expedition, a walk in the park, to name a few situations, demand different styles of dress and require us to be more or less aware of our dress, make it more or less an object of our consciousness.

In bringing embodiment to the fore of his analysis and emphasizing that all human experience comes out of our bodily position, Merleau-Ponty's analysis offers a fruitful starting-point for the analysis of dress as situated bodily practice. Dress is always located spatially and temporally: when getting dressed one orientates oneself/body to the situation, acting in particular ways upon the surfaces of the body in ways that are likely to fit within the established norms of that situation. Thus the dressed body is not a passive object, acted upon by social forces, but actively produced through particular, routine and mundane practices. Moreover, our experience of the body is not as inert object but as the envelope of our being, the site for our articulation of self. Merleau-Ponty's insistence on the embodied nature of subjectivity means that it is crucial to the experience and expression of self, and what could be more visible an aspect of the body than dress? This relationship between the body and identity and between identity and dress has been the subject of many discussions within fashion theory, as well as of some accounts of the body (Davis 1992; Finkelstein 1991; Synnott 1993; Wilson 1985, 1992). However, these accounts have tended not to talk of embodiment and of the ways in which dress constitutes part of the experience of the body and identity. In unifying body/self and in focusing on the experiential dimensions of being located in a body, Merleau-Ponty's work demonstrates how the body is not merely a textual entity produced by discursive practices but is the active and perceptive vehicle of being.

There are, however, a number of problems with Merleau-Ponty's phenomenology. Firstly, he neglects to consider the body as gendered, when in everyday life gender plays a significant part in the way in which individuals, male and female, experience embodiment and come to live in their bodies. Not only is gender in part the product of "techniques of the body" such as those described by Mauss above; the body itself moves through time and space with a sense of itself as gendered. This is illustrated by the ways in which men and women experience the spaces of the public realm differently, as described by Bourdieu. As I have discussed elsewhere (Entwistle 1997, 2000b), the spaces of work are experienced differently by women and men, and this affects the ways in which the body is dressed and presented. Furthermore, as argued by numerous theorists (Berger 1972; McNay 1992; Mulvey 1989; Wolf 1990), women are more likely to be identified with the body than men, and this may generate different experiences of embodiment. It could be argued that women are more likely to develop greater body consciousness and greater awareness of themselves as embodied than men, whose identity is less situated in the body. Tseëlon's (1997) work in this area would seem to testify to this. Secondly, Merleau-Ponty's approach remains philosophical: as a method, it cannot be easily applied to the analysis of the social world. However, Crossley (1995a) and Csordas (1993) see much potential in the works of Goffman and Bourdieu respectively, since both draw some inspiration from phenomenology, but develop approaches to embodiment that are sociological rather than philosophical, and ground their accounts in empirical evidence of actual social practices. I want to explore what each has to say about Goffman and Bourdieu, as well as to suggest the ways in which these two theorists could be applied to the study of the dressed body.

## Dress and Embodied Subjectivity

Crossley (1995a) suggests that there are many other fruitful connections to be made between Goffman (1971, 1972) and Merleau-Ponty (1976, 1981), particularly their insistence on subjectivity as embodied. Furthermore, Goffman's concern with the temporality and spatiality of interaction provides another point of contact with Merleau-Ponty, whose work is concerned with these aspects of perception. In terms of providing an account of embodied subjectivity as experienced within the flow of everyday life, Goffman's concepts have some considerable potential for understanding the dressed body. They enable description and analysis of the way in which individuals, or social actors, come to orientate themselves to the social world and learn to perform in it, and recognize how the body is central to this experience. In Goffman's work, the body is the property of both the individual and the social world: it is the vehicle of identity, but this identity has to be "managed" in terms of the definitions of the social situation, which impose particular ways of being on the body. Thus individuals feel a social and moral imperative to perform their identity in particular ways, and this includes learning appropriate ways of dressing. Like so much bodily behavior, codes of dress come to be taken for granted and are routinely and unreflexively employed, although some occasions, generally formal ones (like weddings and funerals) set tighter constraints around the body, and lend themselves to more conscious reflection on dress. Goffman's work thus adds to Douglas's account of the "two bodies" by bringing embodiment and actual bodily practices into the frame.

In considering the body as central to interaction, his analysis also lends itself to the understanding of the dressed body, and thus to an account of dress in terms of situated bodily practice. Not only does dress form the key link between individual identity and the body, providing the means, or "raw material," for performing identity; dress is fundamentally an inter-subjective and social phenomenon, it is an important link between individual identity and social belonging. Davis (1992: 25) argues that dress frames our embodied self, serving as "a kind of visual metaphor for identity and, as pertains in particular to the open society of the West, for registering the culturally anchored ambivalence that resonates within and among identities." In other words, not only is our dress the visible form of our intentions, but in everyday life dress is the insignia by which we are read and come to read others, however unstable and ambivalent these readings maybe (Campbell 1997). Dress works to "glue" identities in a world where they are uncertain. As Wilson (1985: 12) puts it, "the way in which we dress may assuage that fear by stabilizing our individual identity." This idea is the basis of much subcultural theory on the symbolic work performed by members of subcultures, who, it is argued, deploy cultural artifacts such as dress to mark out the boundaries of their group and register their belonging (Hall and Jefferson 1976; Hebdige 1979; Luck 1992; Willis 1975, 1978).

While Goffman does not discuss the ways dress is used and its role in the "presentation of self in everyday life," his ideas could however be elaborated to discuss the way in which dress is routinely attended to as part of this "presentation of self in everyday life." Most situations, even the most informal, have a code of dress, and these impose particular ways of being on bodies in such a way as to have a social and moral imperative to them. Bell (1976) gives the example of a five-day-old beard, which could not be worn to the theater without censure and disapproval "exactly comparable to that occasioned by dishonorable conduct." Indeed, clothes are often spoken of in moral terms, using words like "faultless," "good," "correct." Few are immune to this social pressure, and most people are embarrassed by certain mistakes of dress, such as finding one's fly undone or discovering a stain on a jacket. Thus, as Bell (1976: 19) puts it, "our clothes are too much a part of us for most of us to be entirely indifferent to their condition: it is as though the fabric were indeed a natural extension of the body, or even of the soul."

Thus in the presentation of self in social interaction, ideas of embarrassment and stigma play a crucial role, and are managed, in part, through dress. Dressed inappropriately for a situation we feel vulnerable and embarrassed, and so too when our dress "fails" us, when in public we find we've lost a button or stained our clothes, or find our fly undone. However, the embarrassment of such mistakes of dress is not simply that of a personal *faux pas,* but the shame of failing to meet the standards required of one by the moral order of the social space. When we talk of someone's "slip showing" we are, according to Wilson (1985: 8), speaking of something "more than slight sartorial sloppiness"; we are actually alluding to "the exposure of something much more profoundly ambiguous and disturbing . . . the naked body underneath the clothes." A commonly cited dream for many people is the experience of suddenly finding oneself naked in a public place: dress, or the lack of it in this case, serves as a metaphor for feelings of shame, embarrassment and vulnerability in our culture, as well as indicating the way in which the moral order demands that the body be covered in some way. These examples illustrate the way in which dress is part of the micro-order of social interaction and intimately connected to our (rather fragile) sense of self, which is, in turn, threatened if we fail to conform to the standards governing a particular social situation. Dress is therefore a crucial dimension in the articulation of personal identity, but not in the sense sometimes argued by theorists, for example, Polhemus (1994) and Finkelstein (1991) who err too much on the side of voluntarism, dress as freely willed, "expressive" and creative. On the contrary, identity is managed through dress in rather more mundane and routine ways, because social pressure encourages us to stay within the bounds of what is defined in a situation as "normal" body and "appropriate" dress. This is not to say that dress has no "creative" or expressive qualities to it, but rather that too much attention and weight has been given to this and too little to the way in which strategies of dress have a strong social and moral dimension to them that serves to constrain the choices people make about what to wear. Tseëlon (1997) has argued that dress choices are made within specific contexts, and provides good examples of the ways in which occasions such as job interviews, weddings, etc. constrain dress choices. Her work therefore points to an important aspect of dress that requires that it be studied as a situated bodily practice. Different occasions, different situations, operate with different codes of dress and bodily demeanor, so that while we may dress unreflexively some of the time (to do the grocery shopping or take the kids to school), at other times we are thoughtful, deliberate and calculating in our dress (I must not wear that white dress to the wedding; I must buy a new suit/jacket/tie for that job interview). Furthermore, dress is also structured in the West (and increasingly beyond) by the fashion system, which, in defining the latest aesthetic, helps to shape trends and tastes that structure our experience of dress in daily life.

Crossley (1995a) suggests that another point of contact between Goffman and Merleau-Ponty is that both take account of space in their analysis. He argues that while Merleau-Ponty is good at articulating spatiality and the perception of it, Goffman provides us with concrete accounts of how this occurs in the social world. Goffman's (1972) sense of space is both social and perceptual, and provides a link between the structuralist/post-structuralist analysis of space delineated by Douglas (1973, 1979) and Foucault (1977) in terms of social order and regulation, and the phenomenological analysis of space as experiential. Moreover, according to Crossley, Goffman takes the analysis of bodily demeanor in social situations further than either Merleau-Ponty and indeed Mauss. Goffman elaborates on Mauss's "techniques of the body," not only recognizing that such things as walking are socially structured, but considering also how walking is not only a part of the interaction order, but serves also to reproduce it. For Goffman, the spaces of the street, the office, the shopping mall, operate with different rules and determine how we present ourselves and how we interact with others. He reminds us of the territorial nature of space, and describes how, when we use space, we have to negotiate crowds, dark quiet spaces, etc. In other words, he articulates the way in which action transforms space. This acknowledgment of space can illuminate the situated nature of dress. If, as I have argued, dress forms part of the micro-social order of most social spaces, when we dress we attend to the norms of particular spatial situations: is there a code of dress we have to abide by? who are we likely to meet? what activities are we likely to perform? how visible do we want to be? (do we want to stand out in the crowd or blend in?), etc. While we may not always be aware of all these issues, we internalize particular rules or norms of dress, which we routinely employ unconsciously. I have argued elsewhere (Entwistle 2000b) that the professional woman is more likely to be conscious of her body and dress in public spaces of work than at home or even in her private office. Space is experienced territorially by professional women, who routinely talk of putting on their jackets to go to meetings and when walking around their workplaces, but taking them off when in the privacy of their offices, the reason being to cover their breasts so as to avoid unsolicited sexual glances from men. Thus spaces impose different ways of being on gendered bodies: women may have to think more carefully about how they appear in public than men, at least in some situations, and the way they experience public spaces such as offices, boardrooms, or quiet streets at night, is likely to be different to the way men experience such spaces. The spaces at work carry different meanings for women, and as a consequence they have developed particular strategies of dress for managing the gaze of others, especially men, in public spaces at work. Their strategies of dress both reflect the gendered nature of the workplace and represent an adaptation to this space in terms of their experience of it. In a similar way, women dressing up for a night out might wear a coat to cover up an outfit, such as a short skirt and skimpy top, which might feel comfortable when worn in a nightclub, but which might otherwise make them feel vulnerable when walking down a quiet street late at night. In this respect, the spaces of the nightclub and the street impose their own structures on the individual and her sense of her body, and she may in turn employ strategies of dress aimed at managing her body in these spaces.

## Dress and Habitus

Bourdieu's (1984, 1989, 1994) work offers another potentially useful sociological analysis of embodiment, and his analysis, which builds a bridge between approaches to the world that prioritize either objective structures or subjective meanings, provides a way of thinking through dress as a situated bodily practice. His notion of the habitus marks an attempt to overcome the either/or of objectivism and subjectivism. As "a system of durable, transposable dispositions" that are produced by the particular conditions of a class grouping, the habitus enables the reproduction of class (and gender) through the active embodiment of individuals who are *structured* by it, as opposed to the passive inscription of power relations on to the body. Thus, the notion of lived practice is not individualistic, it is more than "simply the aggregate of individual behavior" (Jenkins 1992). In this respect, Bourdieu's work elaborates in concrete ways Merleau-Ponty's philosophical approach to embodiment. As Csordas (1993: 137) argues: "to conjoin Bourdieu's understanding of 'habitus' as an unselfconscious orchestration of practices with Merleau-Ponty's notion of the 'pre-objective' suggests that embodiment need not be restricted to the personal or dyadic micro-analysis customarily associated with phenomenology but is relevant as well to social collectivities." In this way, the habitus is the objective outcome of particular social conditions, "structured structures," but these structures cannot be known in advance of their lived practice. The individual social agent develops a "feel for the game," and in the process, comes to interpret, consciously or unconsciously, the 'rules' and improvise around them.

According to McNay (1999), in foregrounding embodiment in his concept of the habitus and in arguing that power is actively reproduced through it, Bourdieu provides for a more complex and nuanced analysis of the body than Foucault whose "passive body" is inscribed with power and an effect of it. The potential of the habitus as a concept for thinking through embodiment is that it provides a link between the individual and the social: the way we come to live in our bodies is structured by our social position in the world, but these structures are only reproduced through the embodied actions of individuals. Once acquired, the habitus enables the generation of practices that are constantly adaptable to the conditions it meets. In terms of dress, the habitus predisposes individuals to particular ways of dressing: for example, the middle-class notion of 'quality not quantity' generally translates into a concern with quality fabrics such as cashmere, leather, silk, which, because of their cost, may mean buying fewer garments. However while social collectivities, class and gender for example, and social situations structure the codes of dress, these are relatively open to interpretation and are only realized through the embodied practice of dress itself. Thus dress is the result of a complex negotiation between the individual and the social and, while it is generally predictable, it cannot be known in advance of the game, since the structures and rules of a situation only set the parameters of dress, but cannot entirely determine it.

Bourdieu's habitus and his theory of practice are useful for overcoming the bias towards texts and towards the discursive body, and have much potential for understanding the dressed body as the outcome of situated bodily practices. The strength of Bourdieu's account applied to dress is that it is not reductive: dress as lived practice is the outcome of neither oppressive social forces on the one hand, nor agency on the other. As McNay (1999: 95) argues, "it yields a more dynamic theory of embodiment than Foucault's work which fails to think through the materiality of the body and thus vacillates between determinism and voluntarism." Bourdieu provides an account of subjectivity that is both embodied, unlike Foucault's passive body and his "technologies of the self," and active in its adaptation of the habitus. As such, it enables an account of dress that does not fall into voluntarism and assume that one is free to self-fashion autonomously. Polhemus's (1994) analysis of "streetstyle" is illustrative of such a voluntarist approach to fashion and dress, which is what has tended to define recent work in this area. In his idea of the "supermarket of style" Polhemus argues that the mixing of youth culture "tribes" in recent years has meant less clearly differentiated boundaries between groups, while his metaphor suggests that young people are now free to choose from a range of styles at will as if they were choices on display in a supermarket. However, such an emphasis on free and creative expression glosses over the structural constraints of class, gender, location, and income that set material boundaries for young people, as well as the constraints at work in a variety of situations that serve to set parameters around dress choice. As McNay (1999: 97) argues, Foucault's later work on technologies of the self rather assumes that identity is open to self-fashioning, and thus fails "to consider fully the recalcitrance of embodied existence to self-fashioning."

However, the notion of the habitus as a dynamic, durable and transposable set of dispositions does allow some sense of agency on the part of individuals. Dress in everyday life cannot be known in advance of practice by examination of the fashion industry or fashion texts. It is a practical negotiation between the fashion system as a structured system, the social conditions of everyday life, such as class, gender and the like, and in addition the "rules" or norms governing particular social situations. Choices over dress are always defined within a particular context: the fashion system provides the "raw material" of our choices but these are adapted within the context of the lived experience of the woman, her class, race and ethnicity, age, occupation and so on. The outcome of this complex interaction cannot be known in advance precisely because the habitus enables improvisation and adaptation to these conditions. It thus enables one to talk about dress as individuals' attempts to orientate themselves to particular circumstances, and thus recognizes the structuring influences of the social world on the one hand, and the agency of the individuals who make choices as to what to wear on the other.

The habitus is also useful for understanding how dress styles are gendered and how gender is actively reproduced through dress. However much gendered identity has been problematized of late, and however much gender roles may have changed, gender is still entrenched within the body styles of men and women, or, as McNay (1999: 98) puts it, "embedded in inculcated, bodily dispositions," which are "relatively involuntary, pre-reflexive." To give a concrete analysis of a particular *field* and return to the example of dress at work, it is apparent that there are gendered styles of dress within the workplace, especially the white-collar and professional workplace. Here we find that the suit is the standard "masculine" dress; and, while women have adopted suits in recent years, theirs differ in many respects from men's. Women have more choices in terms of dress, in that they can, in most workplaces, wear skirts or trousers with their jackets; they have wider choice in terms of color than the usual black, gray, or navy of most male suits for the conventional office, and can decorate them more elaborately with jewelry and other accessories (Entwistle 1997, 2000b; Molloy 1980). However, in order to understand this field one must take account of the historical modes of being in the workplace, as well as the nature of the habitus of this particular field. Significantly, women's adoption of tailored clothes has to do with the orientation of women's bodies to the context of the male workplace and its habitus. In this field, sexuality is deemed inappropriate (it is distracting from production), and the suit, which covers all the male body except for the neck and hands, has become the standard style of dress for men. The meanings of the suit are complex and nuanced, and, while it does not obliterate the sexuality of the male body, it works to obscure, blur or reduce it, as Collier (1998) has argued. In addition, it has come to connote "professional." By examining different styles of dress and corporeality at work, Collier (1998: 34) argues that the male body at work attempts to distance itself from connotations of the body and eroticism: the suit serves the purpose of de-sexualizing the male body, "not in the sense of rendering men in suits beyond erotic attachment (far from it) but rather in terms of erasing the sexed specificity of the individual male body." In other words, rendering "invisible" the male body, the suit hides sexed characteristics, but more importantly, as the standard of dress long established, "this body is normative within the public sphere, it has come to represent neutrality and *dis*embodiment" (Thornton in Collier 1998: 34).

Women's movement into this sphere, as secretaries and later as professionals, required them to adopt a similar uniform to designate them as workers and thus as public as opposed to private figures. However, the feminine body, as Berger (1972), McNay (1992), Mulvey (1989) and

Wolf (1990) have argued is always, potentially at least, a sexual body, and women have not entirely been able to escape this association, despite their challenge to tradition and the acquisition, in part, of sexual equality. In other words, women are still seen as located in the body, whereas men are seen as transcending it. Thus, while a woman can wear a tailored suit much the same as a man, her identity will always be as a "female professional," her body and her gender being outside the norm "masculine" (Entwistle 2000b; Sheppard 1989, 1993). While her suit may work to cover her body and reduce its sexual associations (the jacket is the most crucial aspect of female professional dress, covering the most sexualized zone, the breasts, as was noted above), as I have argued (Entwistle 2000b) it can never entirely succeed, since a woman brings to her dress the baggage of sexual meanings that are entrenched within the culturally established definitions of "femininity." This is not to say that women are embodied and men are not; but that cultural associations do not see men as embodied in the way that women are. In his analysis Collier (1998: 32) argues for consideration of male corporeality at work, suggesting that different styles of masculinity operate in legal practice, but that the "*sexed* specificity of this style has, in contrast to the growing literature on the corporeality of women in the profession, remained largely unexplored." In other words, men's bodies are taken for granted or rendered invisible, in contrast to the attention paid to female bodies at work and in other public arenas. Thus, as he argues, men are embodied, but the experience of embodiment is often left out of accounts of masculinity. He (1998: 32) suggests that this "de-sexing" of men has been dependent "on certain deeply problematic assumptions," and asks, "does this mean that a courtroom consisting solely of men is without, or beyond the erotic? Such an argument would presume, first, that intra-male relations are asexual . . . and secondly, that as sexed beings, men's eroticism is confined to the private, affective sphere."

However, while the male suit can, at least superficially, efface the male body, it cannot obliterate the female body, which is always "feminine" and by association, "sexual." Thus, while more women work, and increasingly in male-defined arenas, break with more traditional images of femininity, "the transformatory impact upon embodied feminine identity and upon the collective subordination of women in society is far from certain" (McNay 1999: 106). McNay (1999: 106) therefore argues that "in pointing to the rootedness of gender divisions in social forms, the concepts of the habitus and 'le sens pratique' serve as a corrective to sociologically naïve claims about the transformation of social and sexual identities." This is due, in part, to the largely unreflexive nature of gender, which, if we draw again on Mauss (1973), is reproduced through "techniques of the body" that come to feel "natural." Bourdieu's notion of the habitus allows for the analysis of such differences in gender in terms of how it is socially reproduced through bodily styles. It enables consideration of how gender is embodied through various techniques, practices, and styles, and how these are repetitive and deeply embedded within unreflective practice. Changes in the social world, such as the changing status of women, are, according to Bourdieu, slow to find their way into the habitus. However, he does also recognize that the habitus is a *relatively* open structure, and one that is constantly, if slowly, modified. Thus, according to McNay (1999: 105), he produces an account of gender identity that is "not a mechanistically determining structure but an open system of dispositions." These dispositions are "durable but not eternal" (Bourdieu, quoted in McNay 1999: 105).

## Conclusion

This article has set out the theoretical framework for a sociology of the dressed body as a situated bodily practice. I have argued that understanding dress requires adopting an approach that acknowledges the body as a social entity and dress as the outcome of both social factors and individual actions. Foucault's work may contribute to a sociology of the body as discursively constituted, but is limited by its inattention to the lived body and its practices, and to the body as the site of the "self." Understanding dress in everyday life requires understanding not just how the body is represented within the fashion system and its discourses on dress, but also how the body is experienced and lived and the role dress plays in the presentation of the body/self. Abandoning Foucault's discursive model of the body does not, however, mean abandoning his entire thesis. This framework, as I have shown, is useful for understanding the structuring influences on the body and the way in which bodies acquire meaning in particular contexts. However, the study of dress as situated practice requires moving between, on the one hand, the discursive and representational aspects of dress and the way the body/dress is caught up in relations of power, and on the other hand, the embodied experience of dress and the use of dress as one means by which individuals orientate themselves to the social world. Dress involves practical actions directed by the body upon the body, which result in ways of being and ways of dressing, such as ways of walking to accommodate high heels, ways of breathing to accommodate a corset, ways of bending in a short skirt, and so on. A sociological account of dress as an embodied and situated practice needs to acknowledge the ways in which both the experience of the body and the various practices of dress are socially structured.

## References

Barthes, R. 1985. *The Fashion System*. London: Cape.
Bell, Q. 1976. *On Human Finery*. London: Hogarth Press.
Berger, J. 1972. *Ways of Seeing*. Harmondsworth: Penguin.

Bourdieu, P. 1984. *Distinction: A Social Critique of the Judgement of Taste*. Cambridge, MA: Harvard University Press.

——. 1989. *Outline of a Theory of Practice*. Cambridge: Cambridge University Press.

——. 1994. "Structures, Habitus and Practices." In P. Press (ed.), *The Polity Reader in Social Theory*, Cambridge: Polity Press.

Butler, J. 1990. *Gender Trouble: Feminism and the Subversion of Identity*. London: Routledge.

——. 1993. *Bodies That Matter*. London: Routledge.

Campbell, C. 1997. "When the Meaning Is Not a Message: A Critique of the Consumption as Communication Thesis." In M. Nava, A. Blake, I. MacRury, and B. Richards (eds), *Buy this Book: Studies in Advertising and Consumption*, London: Routledge.

Collier, R. 1998. "'Nutty Professors', 'Men in Suits' and 'New Entrepreneurs': Corporeality, Subjectivity and Change in the Law School and Legal Practice." *Social and Legal Studies*, 7 (1): 27–53.

Crossley, N. 1995a. "Body Techniques, Agency and Inter-corporality: On Goffman's Relations in Public." *Sociology* 129 (1): 133–49.

——. 1995b. "Merleau-Ponty, the Elusive Body and Carnal Sociology." *Body and Society*, 1 (1): 43–63.

——. 1996. "Body/Subject, Body/Power: Agency, Inscription and Control in Foucault and Merleau-Ponty." *Body and Society*, 2 (2): 99–116.

Csordas, T. J. 1993. "Somatic Modes of Attention." *Cultural Anthropology*, 8 (2): 135–56.

——. 1996. "Introduction: The Body As Representation and Being-in-the-world." In T. J. Csordas (ed.), *Embodiment and Experience: The Existential Ground of Culture and Self*. Cambridge: Cambridge University Press.

Davis, F. 1992. *Fashion, Culture and Identity*. Chicago: University of Chicago Press.

Derrida, J. 1976. *Of Grammatology*. Baltimore, MD: Johns Hopkins University Press.

Diamond, I. and L. Quinby (eds). 1988. *Feminism and Foucault: Reflections on Resistance*. Boston: Northeastern University Press.

Douglas, M. 1970. *Natural Symbols: Explorations in Cosmology*. London: Barrie & Rockliff.

——. 1979. *Implicit Meanings: Essays in Anthropology*. London: Routledge.

——. 1984. *Purity and Danger: An Analysis of the Concept of Pollution and Taboo*. London: Routledge and Kegan Paul.

Eco, U. 1986. "Lumbar Thought." *Travels in Hyperreality*. Orlando, FL: Harcourt Brace Jovanovich.

Entwistle, J. 1997. "Power Dressing and the Fashioning of the Career Woman." In M. Nava, I. MacRury, A. Blake, and B. Richards (eds), *Buy this Book: Studies in Advertising and Consumption*. London: Routledge.

— —. 2000a. *The Fashioned Body: Fashion, Dress and Modern Society*. Cambridge: Polity.

— —. 2000b. "Fashioning the Career Woman: Power Dressing as a Strategy of Consumption." In M. Talbot and M. Andrews (eds), *All the World and Her Husband: Women and Consumption in the Twentieth Century*. London: Cassell.

Entwistle, J. and E. Wilson. 1998. "The Body Clothed." In *A 100 Years of Art and Fashion* (catalog). London: Hayward Gallery.

Finkelstein, J. 1991. *The Fashioned Self*. Cambridge: Polity.

Foucault, M. 1977. *Discipline and Punish*. Harmondsworth: Penguin.

— —. 1980. "Body/Power." In C. Gordon (ed.), *Power/Knowledge: Selected Interviews and Other Writings 1972–77*. New York: Pantheon Books.

— —. 1986. *The History of Sexuality: Volume Three, The Care of the Self*. London: Penguin.

Freeman, C. 1993. "Designing Women: Corporate Discipline and Barbados's Off-shore Pink Collar Sector." *Cultural Anthropology*, 8 (2).

Gamman, L. and M. Makinen. 1994. *Female Fetishism: A New Look*. London: Lawrence and Wishart.

Giddens, A. 1991. *Modernity and Self-Identity: Self and Society in the Late Modern Age*. Cambridge: Polity.

Goffman, E. 1971. *The Presentation of Self in Everyday Life*. London: Penguin.

— —. 1972. *Relations in Public*. Harmondsworth: Pelican Books.

Hall, S. and T. Jefferson. (eds) 1976. *Resistance Through Rituals: Youth Subcultures in Post-war Britain*. London: Hutchinson.

Haug, F. (ed.) 1987. *Female Sexualization*. London: Verso.

Hebdige, D. 1979. *Subculture: The Meaning of Style*. London: Methuen.

Hollander, A. 1993. *Seeing Through Clothes*. Berkeley, CA: University of California Press.

Jenkins, R. 1992. *Pierre Bourdieu*. London: Routledge.

Kuhn, A. 1988. "The Body and Cinema: Some Problems for Feminism." In S. Sheridan (ed.), *Grafts: Feminist Cultural Criticism*. London: Verso.

Kunzle, D. 1982. *Fashion and Fetishism: A Social History of the Corset, Tight-lacing and Other Forms of Body-Sculpture in the West*. Totowa, NJ: Rowan and Littlefield.

Luck, K. 1992. "Trouble in Eden, Trouble with Eve: Women, Trousers and Utopian Socialism in Nineteenth Century America." In J. Ash and E. Wilson (eds), *Chic Thrills: A Fashion Reader*. London: Pandora.

Lurie, A. 1981. *The Language of Clothes*. New York: Random House.

Mauss, M. 1973. "Techniques of the Body." *Economy and Society*, 2 (1): 70–89.

McNay, L. 1992. *Foucault and Feminism: Power, Gender and the Self*. Cambridge: Polity Press.

— —. 1999. "Gender, Habitus and the Field: Pierre Bourdieu and the Limits of Reflexivity." *Theory, Culture and Society*, 16 (1): 95–117.

Merleau-Ponty, M. 1976. *The Primacy of Perception*. USA: Northwestern University Press.

— —. 1981. *The Phenomenology of Perception*. London: Routledge and Kegan Paul.

Molloy, J. T. 1980. *Women: Dress for Success*. New York: Peter H. Wyden.

Mulvey, L. 1989. *Visual and Other Pleasures*. London: Macmillan.

Polhemus, T. 1988. *Bodystyles*. Luton: Lennard.

— —. 1994. *Streetstyle*. London: Thames and Hudson.

Polhemus, T. and L. Proctor. 1978. *Fashion and Anti-fashion: An Anthology of Clothing and Adornment*. London: Cox & Wyman.

Ramazanoglu, C. (ed.) 1993. *Up Against Foucault: Explorations of Some Tensions between Foucault and Feminism*. London: Routledge.

Roberts, H. 1977. "The Exquisite Slave: The Role of Clothes in the Making of the Victorian Woman." *Signs*, 2 (3): 554–69.

St Martin, L. and Gavey, N. 1996. "Women Body Building: Feminist Resistance and/or Femininity's Recuperation." *Body and Society*, 2 (4): 45–57.

Schulze, L. 1990. "On the Muscle." In J. Gaines and C. Herzog (eds), *Fabrications: Costume and the Female Body*. London: Routledge.

Sheppard, D. L. 1989. "Organisations, Power and Sexuality: The Image and Self-Image of Women Managers." In J. E. A. Hearn (ed.), *The Sexuality of the Organisation*. London: Sage.

— —. 1993. "Women Managers' Perceptions of Gender and Organizational Life." In A. J. Mills and P. Tancred (eds), *Gendering Organizational Analysis*. London: Sage.

Synnott, A. 1993. *The Body Social: Symbolism, Self and Society*. London: Routledge.

Tseëlon, E. 1997. *The Masque of Femininity*. London: Sage.

Turner, B. 1985. *The Body and Society: Explorations in Social Theory*. Oxford: Basil Blackwell.

Turner, T. 1996. "Bodies and Anti-bodies: Flesh and Fetish in Contemporary Social Theory." In T. Csordas (ed.), *Embodiment and Experience: The Existential Ground of Culture and Self*. Cambridge: Cambridge University Press.

Willis, P. 1975. "The Expressive Style of a Motor-bike Culture." In Benthall and Polhemus (eds), *The Body as a Medium of Expression*. London: Allen Lane.

— —. 1978. *Profane Culture*. London: Routledge & Kegan Paul.

Wilson, E. 1985. *Adorned in Dreams: Fashion and Modernity*. London: Virago.

— —. 1992. "The Postmodern Body." In J. Ash and E. Wilson (eds), *Chic Thrills: A Fashion Reader*. London: Pandora.

Wolf, N. 1990. *The Beauty Myth: How Images of Beauty Are Used Against Women*. London: Vintage.

*Fashion Theory*, Volume 4, Issue 3, pp.349–358
Reprints available directly from the Publishers.
Photocopying permitted by licence only.

# A Note: Yinka Shonibare: Dress Tells the Woman's Story[1]

**Janice M. Cheddie**

Yinka Shonibare's *Five Under/Garments* (1992) and *How Does A Girl Like You Get To Be A Girl Like You* (1995) illustrate the ways in which contemporary artists have used clothes within their work as vehicles to explore narratives of desire and memory and to reflect on the processes of colonial commodity production. A number of themes emerge within Shonibare's work: revealing and concealing; the body in pain; and counter-narratives to the hegemonic discourses of modernity.

- **Revealing and Concealing:** While clothes function on the level of visual communication and signification, they are also commodities. Like all commodities clothes are constructed on a series of narratives, which reveal and conceal their history of production, trade relations and cultural use. Shonibare draws upon these narratives, inherent in the production and display of clothes, to explore issues concerning the body, cultural memory, loss, colonial commodity production and gendered and racialized identities.

- **The Body In Pain:** Shonibare has to engage the audience in a dialogue about the body; furthermore within this dialogue he has touched on the theme of "the body in pain." Shonibare's Victorian garments reference through the absent (female) body the relationship between pain and pleasure inscribed within the sexual economy of the corset, while also exploring femininity as a performed gendered identity.
- **Counter-Memories/Alternative Histories:** Shonibare's re-making of garments of the Victorian lady references the various colonial trade routes and relationships that underpin the manufacture and readings of the wax-printed cloth in the West.
- **Absences/Presences: Absent Bodies/Empty Dresses:** By removing the physical body and presenting the viewer with a shell, Shonibare suggests to the viewer that the social meaning of the body is constructed within a system of visual signification rather than on the material body itself. In drawing our attention to the human body as something that is read and socially constructed Shonibare seeks to disrupt common-sense notions concerning cultural and sexual difference.

If dress tells the woman's story, exactly what story are Yinka Shonibare's installations *Five Under/Garments and Much More (1995)* and *How Does A Girl Like You Become a Girl Like You (1992)* seeking to tell us? These installations present the viewer with wax-printed cloths, fashioned into the attire of a Victorian bourgeois woman. By presenting the viewer with exquisitely designed garments, Shonibare is immediately disrupting the notions of authorship that exist in contemporary Western fashion as opposed to traditional costume. Within the western signifying system of fashion these wax-printed materials are positioned as a signifier of ethnic identity—i.e. African "traditional" costume equals unchanging and un-designed. By tailoring these garments in the manner of labor-intensive, highly designed costumes, Shonibare's installations disrupt the notions of ethnic-traditional-craft-primitive-intuitive, by placing them firmly within the signifying system of Western fashion of designed-authored-creative-sophisticated artifacts.

Shonibare continues this removal of associations with notions of ethnic identity. Firstly, Shonibare absents the body, with its markings of racial and cultural otherness; this strategy of removing the wearer draws the viewer's attention to the relationship between costume/fashion, gender, authenticity, artifice and cultural identity. Secondly, Shonibare exposes the viewer to the ways in which these wax-printed cloths have entered Western European and North American cultures as signifiers of "African" and "ethnic" while remaining within African fashion systems as valued

**Figure 1**

Yinka Shonibare. "How Does a Girl Like You Get to be a Girl Like You?" 1995. Installation of three costumes of wax print cotton textiles. Tailored by Sian Lewis. Approx. height 168cm (66in). SHO 02. Courtesy of the Stephen Friedman Gallery.

items because of their removal from local production and custom. This mistaking of the sign for the signifier, within Western systems of representation, is further confused with the taking up of these clothes by members of the African diaspora as a symbol of racial identification, authenticity and solidarity with continental African peoples.

Shonibare's interrogations of these issues are centered within the installations on the structure and design of the cloth itself. The manufacture of wax-printed batiks resulted from a hybrid process, whose production techniques originated in Indonesia, but were taken by Dutch traders to Holland in the nineteenth century. The original market for these Dutch-designed batiks was as competition against the locally-made batiks of Indonesia. These Dutch-produced cloths, however, were not popular in Indonesia, owing to their inferior quality, but found favor in the West African market . Thus the cloths we now think of as African materials are the products of Dutch and British (Manchester) design for the West African market. Even the designs and motifs on the materials draw upon this hybridity: "... whoever was responsible for advising the Haarlem engravers was drawing upon Indonesian and ancient Egyptian visual sources, West African proverbial and educational interests, and the Dutch countryside; and all rendered in a style derived from Indonesian batik."[2] Rather than their being the product of an African cultural identity, Shonibare exposes a complex history of colonialism, trade relations, technologies of production and fashion that are inscribed within the techniques, designs and consumption of these cloths. The question that Shonibare poses to the viewer is: Exactly what is it within these cloths that signals notions of ethnicity for the Western viewer?

The installations *Five Under/Garments . . .* and *How Does A Girl . . .* are not acts of colonial mimicry on the part of the desiring colonial subject seeking to gain entry into the closed Western system of power and subjection. But rather, within Shonibare's work, cultural identities are revealed through the associations of these cloths with "ethnic" identity as artifice and a part of a masquerade that constructs gendered identities not only as performative roles but also as racial identities. Shonibare's work seeks to examine the ways in which these Victorian garments of the West are not merely operating within a Western-defined fashion system but also function in Shonibare's own words, as "ethnic English attire,"[3] both within and outside the West.

It is on the level of the complexity of these overlapping and intermingling relationships that the multiple layers of the costume in *How Does A Girl Like You Get To Be a Girl Like You* begin to operate. Shonibare through the construction of this dress begins to call attention to the relationships between gender, cultural identity, authenticity and artifice. Shonibare then leads the viewer on to the relationship between costume and identity. Furthermore, by fashioning these dresses out of Western-produced, ethnically identified wax-printed cloths, Shonibare begins an examination of the intersection between the sexual economies of empire, fashion and desire.

The cultural identity inscribed within the dress is constructed not through the presence of the wearer and its bodily symbols of racial difference, i.e. skin color, but rather through the masquerade. Within contemporary cultural theory masquerade is that which constructs gender roles as a "production of the self as the thing most expected . . . but marking it as fake."[4] Within the concept of the masquerade as a performance of female gender roles, the woman performs the culturally defined role of the feminine by exaggerating notions of femininity, through clothes and adornment, marking femininity as artifice rather than a natural attribute. Femininity is a mask that is worn by the woman to draw attention to the production of femininity as an image, not constructed by individual women but by the codes and conventions of history and culture. Far from being a passive acceptance of the notions of the feminine as natural, within the concept of the masquerade the woman turns herself into the image most expected, a performed identity that reveals itself as a construction.

Shonibare's work opens up a discourse on the ways in which theories of the masquerade can be used not only to draw attention to the ways in which clothes and adornment construct gendered identities but also racialized identities. By employing the concept of the masquerade, Shonibare begins a dialogue concerned with the ways in which the image of the Victorian woman was constructed as a racial and sexual identity.

The "lady" as a model of femininity moved in the nineteenth century from being a closed elite category dependent on aristocratic birth and privilege to an ideological category by which all women could and would be judged.[5] As a discourse of femininity, the Victorian image of the "lady" was premised on the woman's attaining four crucial elements—purity, piety, domesticity and fidelity. If there were women who were pure, faithful, domesticated and pious, then equally there were women who were not. Thus, the image of the woman as lady is an image that is also based on performance. "One acts like a lady, tries to be a lady, but a woman is never really a lady." A state of becoming rather than being.[6]

The construction of this image of femininity operated both within the metropolitan centers and their colonial margins as a discourse of control and regulation of female sexuality, but also as a way of constructing nation and nationhood. Foucault in his *History of Sexuality* (1978) locates the formation of a bourgeois body, premised on sexuality, hygiene and health, as an important building-block in the formation of nineteenth-century

**Figure 2**
Yinka Shonibare. "How Does a Girl Like You Get to be a Girl Like You?" 1995. Installation of three costumes of wax print cotton textiles. Tailored by Sian Lewis. Approx. height 168cm (66in). SHO 02. Courtesy of the Stephen Friedman Gallery.

Janice M. Cheddie

Figure 3
Yinka Shonibare. "Five Under Garments and Much More" 1995. African fabric, Rigilene, fishing line, interlining. Tailored by Sian Lewis. 95 × 130cm (37 × 51in) circumference each. SHO 04. Courtesy of Stephen Friedman Gallery.

racism. The image of the Victorian woman as "pure" and "virtuous" was an important discourse in the nineteenth-century processes of empire nation-building. It is in this sense that the image of the white Victorian lady is a performed racialized identity.

By placing the Victorian woman's dress within the signifying system of colonial expansion and trade, and by uncovering the complex history of the wax-printed cloth, Shonibare leads the viewer in questioning the construction of the image of femininity of the Victorian lady as a racialized image. Shonibare leads the viewer towards this reading through a deconstruction of the Victorian woman as a sign of colonial expansion.

In recognizing that the status of being a lady is dependent on the signifiers of attire, Shonibare's installation seeks to disrupt its most prominent signifier, the physically constricting dress of the bourgeois "lady." By constructing the Victorian garments out of a brightly colored and printed cloth, Shonibare undermines this image, which is based on notions of bourgeois discretion, understatement and modesty, placing within its system of reference material that operates as its antithesis— brightly colored "ethnically," and within the Western signifying system positioned as a symbol of the "primitive" cloth. Richard Dyer in his analysis of the Hollywood film *Jezebel* (1938), in a scene where the white heroine Julie (Bette Davis) refuses to wear a white dress, a symbol of purity, to a ball and instead decides to wear a red satin dress, in his analysis of the differing racialized and sexualized associations of the codes of dress, highlights the ways in which the preference for and wearing of bright colors is associated with black femininity and sexuality:

> The immediate scandal is not just the refusal to conform and uphold the celebration of virginity that the white dress code represents, but the sexual connotations of the dress itself, satin and red . . . This is the dress of Julie's (Bette Davis) that her black maid Zette (Theresa Harris) . . . most covets, and after the ball, Julie gives it to her. It is precisely this *colorfulness* that, stereotyping informs us, draws Zette—the dress is "marked" as colored, a definite bold color heightened by a flashy fabric, just as black representation is. Thus what appears to be symbolism (white for virginity, color for sex) within a universally applicable communication circuit becomes ethnically specific.[7]

It is precisely these racially coded signifiers that Shonibare's dresses disrupt. Within Shonibare's installations, the inscribing of the Victorian garments within a racialized code of gaudiness highlights the ways in which these garments operate within a sexual economy of desire. Far from being an expression of "passionlessness,"[8] these costumes speak of sexuality, desire and empire in overt and coded ways. Shonibare's installation also seeks to draw the viewers' attention to the ways in which Victorian costume sought to conceal the sexuality of the bourgeois woman while encasing her body within a fetishized object of desire and sexual display.

The image of Victorian femininity places as central to its appearance an assumed transparent relationship between the dress and the wearer—hence, the emphasis on the appearance of the bourgeois woman as one that is modest, discreet and understated, and on her dress as outward symbol of her purity and piety and the bourgeois woman's position within the public sphere of Victorian England. Shonibare, aware of this linking between the outward state and the internal state of the soul, deliberately sets out to expose the contradictions of this stated relationship between the exterior and interior woman as inscribed upon the dress.

Through the use of this wax-printed cloth and its associations with being gaudy and by association primitive, Shonibare exposes the inherent economy of sexual desire and fetishism in the dress. *How Does A Girl . . .* draws attention to the autoerotic nature of the corset and its tight whalebone structure, which accentuates and contorts the body. Within the contemporary sexual economy of desire and display the corset has remained an item of sexual display and performance. Its very restricted nature as a signifier of pain and aesthetic and sexual pleasure remains a recurring motif re-acted within sado-masochist economies of desire. These erotic elements are also displayed through the costume's bustle which emphasizes and enlarges the white woman's bottom. Yet these are the very same historical discourses that simultaneously fetishized the white woman's bottom and ridiculed the size of the black woman's as obscene and ugly: witness the exhibiting of Sarah Bartman, a.k.a. "the Hottentot Venus," in the nineteenth-century colonial centers of Western Europe. The North American writer Lillian Smith relates how the Southern American white woman was taught to envision her own maturing sexual body within a racial system of segregation of permissions and denials: "Now parts of your body are segregated areas which you must stay away from and keep others away from. These areas you touch only when necessary. In other words, you cannot associate with them any more than you can associate freely with colored children."[9]

These system of permissions and refusals were inscribed contradictorily within the design of the dress—contradictions that are revealed through the dress's tight bodice, which restricted access to the woman's breast and completely concealed the woman's legs, stomach and hips while enlarging the size of her bottom. Within Shonibare's framing, the use of the brightly colored wax-printed material disrupts the Victorian bourgeois image of purity. In displacing the ideal of the Victorian woman as pure, Shonibare disrupts the sexual economy signified by the image of the bourgeois Victorian woman and reveals it as a system that operates around the binary of bad girls and nice ladies.

In the placing of these factory-produced wax-printed cloths, products of European colonial relations, within the construction of the bourgeois Victorian woman's dress, Shonibare draws our attention to the ways in which this image of femininity was positioned within the signifying system of colonial relationships and power.

## Notes

1. This article is an extract from "The Will to Adorn" an interactive web-based project commissioned by Aavaa (The African and Asian visual artists archive, University of East London).
2. Picton (1995: 28).
3. Telephone conversation with author, January 1998.
4. Jones (1998: 35).
5. Armstrong and Tennenhouse (1991: 1–38).
6. Fox (1977: 809). I have discussed the importance of this image in relationship to the construction of Anglo–American black femininity in my unpublished Ph.D. thesis (Cheddie 1995).
7. Dyer (1988: 56).
8. I have taken this term from Cott (1978).
9. Smith 1961 [1949], quoted in Gaines (1992).

## References

Armstrong, Nancy and Leonard Tennenhouse. 1991. "The Literature of Conduct, the Conduct of Literature and the Politics of Desire: An Introduction." In *The Ideology of Conduct: Essays on Literature and The History of Sexuality*. London and New York: Methuen.

Cheddie, Janice M. 1995. "Arresting Black Beauty: Race, Fashion and Black Femininity." Unpublished Ph.D. thesis, University of Sunderland.

Cott, Nancy. 1978. "Passionlessness: An Interpretation of Victorian Sexual Ideology, 1790–1850." *Signs: Journal of Women in Culture and Society*, Vol. 4 No. 2: 219–36.

Dyer, Richard. 1988. "Nice Girls: Social Control of Women Through a Value Construct." *Signs: Journal of Women in Culture and Society*, Vol. 2 No. 4: 809.

Gaines, Jane. 1992. "Competing Glances," *New Formations*, Spring.

Jones, Amelia. 1998. "Tracing the Subject with Cindy Sherman," in *Cindy Sherman: Retrospective, Essays by Amanda Cruz, Elizabeth A.T. Smith, Amelia Jones, Museum of Contemporary Art, Chicago*. Thames and Hudson, pp. 33–54.

Picton, John. 1995. *The Art of African Textiles: Technology, Tradition and Lurex*. Barbican Art Gallery. London: Lund Humphries Publishers.

Smith, Lillian. 1961 [1949]. *Killers of The Dream*. New York and London: W. W. Norton.

*Fashion Theory*, Volume 4, Issue 3, pp.359–368
Reprints available directly from the Publishers.
Photocopying permitted by licence only.
© 2000 Berg. Printed in the United Kingdom.

**Reviewed by
Steven Zdatny**

# Book Review

**Good Hair Days: A History of British Hairstyling,
Caroline Cox. Quartet Books, London, 1999.**

Because hair is so often considered one of the "trivialities of femininity," (1) writes the author Caroline Cox in her introduction, it has seldom received serious study. That is certainly not to say that hair has been ignored for its social and psychological implications. Cox cites, for example, a "phrenologist of some repute" who lectured regularly in 1912 on the subject, "How to Tell Character from Hair," (4) and the 1996 article in the *Globe*, entitled "Di: Hair Own Story," that "purported to chart Princess Diana's state of mind and growing maturity through her changing hair-styles . . ." (5) Cox herself proposes something entirely more sober, almost academic; that is, to describe the unfolding of British hair fashions over the last one hundred fifty years and to tell us something of the deeper signification of the poofs, curls, waves, chignons, and assorted cuts that pass along the surface of social convention. The narrative proceeds along several different tracks: the history of the hairdressing profession itself, of styles, capillary technology, and notable personalities —all the while chasing the question of meaning.

The first chapter, subtitled "Hair and Femininity," picks up the story in the nineteenth century, at a moment of what Cox (questionably) labels "a moment of increasing disenfranchisement of women." (15) We find ourselves in the Victorian era, when women were restricted to "private spaces" and "upswept hair" stood as the symbol of sexual repression. (18) The repressed and corseted Victorians were followed by the more "extravagant" Edwardians, whose hair advertised the period's love of "conspicuous consumption," a tale told in the "complex language" of shells, ribbons, flowers, feathers, diamonds, and other pricey knick-knacks. Indeed, Cox tells us, important functions in High Society generated such a huge demand for the services of a hairdresser "that many women had to have their hair dressed . . . two days in advance," only to spend the nights preceeding the *soirée* "sitting up in a chair in order not to crush the elaborate coiffure." (20) And you thought the rich had it easy.

While the business of women's hair boomed, affairs in the barbershop dragged. Hair clippers first appeared in 1879. In 1895, King Gillette introduced the safety razor. These inventions ushered in an era of short hair and smooth chins that men could administer at home. (Does that mean men were being driven into society's "private spaces"?) Cox suggests that, as the barbershop's practical function dwindled, it picked up an ideological role. "Barbershops," she writes, "were, and to some extent still are, deliberately anti-feminine institutions asserting an active male sexuality, the 'something for the weekend' aesthetic." Whatever this means, it sounds sinister. What's worse, there was no profit in it.

Cox's history then skips to that seminal moment in the twentieth-century history of hair, the Bob. The adoption by grown-up women of this traditional cut for little girls marked more than an important moment in fashion. It looked rather like a social revolution, "the physiological expression of feminity in crisis." (51) The Bob became the emblem of the "new woman," the image of "serpentine slimness," youthful, un-chaperoned, un-married, un-chained. Cox quotes Mary Trasko, who related her own experience:

> All the young women at the office were having their hair cut short . . . my mother and I went to the hairdresser's on Ardour Street, where we sat at the end of a long queue of women who, like us, were patiently waiting to let down their beautiful long hair. An hour

later, with hats too large for our diminished heads, feeling very self-conscious, anxious to be home where we could make a minute, pitiless examination of our changed appearance, we emerged as new women. (44)

The Bob, which after all required going out and *buying* a haircut, was also evidence of a consumer revolution. For once it was not the old society matrons setting the pace in fashion, but *young* women, even young working-class women, who now had the right and the means to aspire to a measure of stylish distinction. Cox adds that the Bob, and the auxiliary services that surrounded it (shampoos, perms, coloring), led to an effective modernization of the hairdressing profession and a general "levelling up of standards" in the salons. (57)

Modernization was accompanied by the increasing presence of women in the salons as providers of services, as well as clients. At the turn of the century, Cox reports, only one employee in ten was a woman, "but as cashiers and assistants rather than stylists." (71) The absence of the fair sex reflected the widespread belief that hairdressing was not fit employment for a woman. Concern with "the delicacy attached to gender relations" helped to keep women haircutters out of barbershops, where they would be forced to have intimate contact with men. It also affected what the French called *salons mixtes*. The Don Hairdressing and Toilet Salon in Brighton, for instance, felt compelled to create a "ladies' annexe," instead of simply having "a shop where" as the *Hairdressers' Weekly Journal* put it, "gentlemen might purchase at the same counter, which may not be agreeable or pleasant to the fair sex." (68)

Like so many old proprieties, this one crumbled under the weight of the First World War. Cox writes of the thousands of hairdressers called to military duty, a professional crisis "exacerbated by the deportation and internment of many foreign hairdressers as aliens and undesirables . . ." (71) Cox approvingly quotes a survey taken by the London Guild of Hairdressers before 1914 concluding that 97 per cent of local master hairdressers were foreign-born. This figure is hard to believe, but no matter. Anti-German hysteria invaded the salons, where placards appeared asking, "Is your hairdresser English? If not—why not?" The *Hairdressers' Weekly Journal* reported on the travails of "five Germans and one Hungarian [who] were recently taken into custody in Eastbourne. One of them (a German) who had resided in the town nearly twenty years, had been employed by a local hairdresser, and had always conducted himself in a highly respectable manner. The provisions of the law, however, had to be carried out to the letter. An armed escort (six men and a sergeant) arrived at Eastbourne, and the prisoners were escorted from the Town Hall to the Railway Station." (73) A German hairdresser in Edinburgh was rumored to have been arrested and shot as a spy, a story he vehemently denied. In any case, the war opened salon doors to lady hairdressers. This stimulated the usual fears that standards would fall and, more critically, that the additional competition would "cheapen labor and lower wages." (74) As the century progressed, however, lady hairdressers became commonplace without bringing catastrophe to the trade.

One of the more fascinating aspects of the Hair Story, of a piece with the twentieth-century cult of celebrity, is the emergence of hairdresser "stars," which development Cox examines in her second chapter, "The Hairdresser as Guru." Their rise to cultural prominence is all the more surprising in view of hairdressers' low profile and status at the end of the last century, at a moment when even privileged hair, for the vast majority of occasions, was the domain of valets and ladies' maids. (64) Still, the phenomenon of celebrity *coiffeurs* was not exactly new. Léonard, hairdresser to Marie Antoinette, became famous for the huge, elaborate hair sculptures with which he adorned the heads at the court of Louis XVI. Similarly, at the end of the nineteenth century Marcel Grateau built a fortune and an international reputation on his invention of a new technique for waving women's hair. It nonetheless remains true that the twentieth century can count an unparalleled number of such "stars," who wielded unprecedented influence in the new consumer culture.

Cox makes it clear that if certain characters stood out from the mass of their colleagues, it was also the case that the hairdressing trade as a whole was undergoing a significant professionalization. Manuals and articles in the *Hairdressers' Weekly Journal* began to instruct readers on various aspects of professional comportment: how to demonstrate "class," how to dress and to take care of hands and wrists. Gilbert Foan's *The Art and Craft of Hairdressing* (1931) taught students that "undue intimacy or familiarity must be avoided." It advised the novice hairdresser "to read good books, to follow intelligently the news in the newspapers, so that he may be able to discuss with his client not only topical questions, but things which are more important and fundamental." (78) Professional training, either by way of apprenticeship or in the growing number of technical colleges, became more regularized and thorough.

High above the crowd of competent professionals soared the international celebrities of hairdressing, who are the real focus of this chapter, and standing above them all was the incomparable Antoine. His story has been retold many times: the talented young immigrant to France from Poland, the pathbreaking sumptuousness of his salon on the rue Cambon, just behind the Ritz Hotel, the invention of the "Joan of Arc" cut, the use of radical ("Bulgarian") hair colors, the collaboration with Coco Chanel, the long, painted fingernails and white suits, the "Glass House" with its crystal sarcophagus for a bed. Antoine's most famous client was Wallis Simpson, the Duchess of Windsor, whose fashion demands were extraordinary even by the standards of wretched excess common in Antoine's world.

Antoine became a cultural icon largely through his unmatched genius for self-promotion; but he made his mark on the profession by abandoning "nineteenth-century techniques of curling, rolling, twisting and frizzing" clients' hair (91). Instead he created individualized styles. He called it "physiognomical hairdressing"; that is, matching the cut to the woman's individual physiognomy. And he considered each coiffure a work of art. As Antoine ran out of steam in the 1950s (the outbreak of war in 1939 had fortunately found him in the United States, where he spent the duration), he was succeeded by others. His protégé Alexandre "de Paris" remains foremost among them.

British hairdressers, says Cox, even the best-known, had long been intimidated by their French counterparts. Beginning in the 1950s, however, a number of them rose to national prominence. One, Vidal Sassoon, became an international figure. Raymond, who also called himself Mr Teasie Weasie, was the campest of the lot. "The majority of women," he wrote in his autobiography, thought that unless you were both queer and French you could not possibly be a good hairdresser." (94) So he permed his hair, wore sandals, painted his toenails, varnished his fingernails, and affected a French accent. Cox labels him the "Liberace of hairdressing," a "parody of self-presentation." (111) He was also, like Antoine, a tyrant in the salon:

> The problem with most women is that they cannot visualize a hairstyle, so the only answer is to be firm. Tell them they must either agree with what you decide or you will not do their hair. If a woman chatters endlessly I shut her up with a single comment: 'Talk is cheap, madam,' I say, 'but money buys houses, so let's get on with it . . .' I finish off the job that God left unfinished. (112)

Raymond's outrageousness caused a reaction among more serious-minded British coiffeurs, like Freddie French. The real turning-point for British hairdressing, however, arrived with Vidal Sassoon, whom Cox describes as "a member of the revolutionary set," the cultural avant-garde of the 1960s. In his impact, although less in his personal style, Sassoon was a figure akin to Antoine. His career sailed high on the wings of the *Zeitgeist*. Where Raymond built his notoriety on the "poodle cut," Sassoon adopted a modernist aesthetic, "with Bauhaus principles at its core . . ." (123) As he told the designer, Mary Quant: "I'm going to cut the hair like you cut material. No fuss. No ornamentation. Just a neat, clean, swinging line." (120) In an age, much like the twenties, when youth and naturalness defined the feminine ideal, Sassoon's cuts aimed not for sculpted stability but for movement and casualness. These ideas made him the toast of "Swinging London." And soon Hollywood. With his public cropping of Mia Farrow, on the soundstage of *Rosemary's Baby* (and for $5,000), the hairdresser became a performance artist.

Cox's chapter on the "hairdresser as guru" displays both the book's best qualities and its shortcomings. The author writes with style and wit. She deploys amusing vignettes, ironical quotations, and apt illustrations to wonderful effect. But Cox intends her study of hairdressing history to be something more than merely diverting. She also wants to offer us a study in cultural analysis, and in this the chapter succeeds rather less well. Aside from small errors of historical fact—for example, twice placing Léonard (and, by implication, his patroness, Marie Antoinette) in the wrong century—and a disconcerting tendency for the narrative to jump back and forth between subjects, Cox does not really fulfill her promise to take us deeper into the meaning of it all.

Her history of hairstyles focuses on a series of evocative types: from repressed Victorians, extravagant Edwardians, and bobbed flappers, through the retrograde 1950s and into the "swinging sixties," whose youthful, girlish aesthetic is so reminiscent of the first postwar era. Yet despite Cox's premise, that hairstyles are "ritualistic and creative behavior which says much about ourselves," (1) and despite the occasional stab at deconstruction and gender analysis, she never lingers very long on the relationship between "ritual behavior" and social reality. Her presentation raises obvious questions: Is there some intimate link between aesthetics and context? Between dominant styles and the condition of those who wear them? Are women "freer" when they have short hair? Do they *feel* freer somehow? Why is it, apart from their intrinsic talent, that the coiffures of Antoine and Sassoon made such a splash, while Raymond remained a campy second-rater and the great mass of hairdressers labored in perfect historical obscurity?

To take a case in point, as Cox herself notes, in spite of the fact that women have played an increasingly large role in the profession, with a few notable exceptions the celebrities of hairdressing have all been men. (93) Yet while the author takes note of the "glass ceiling" within the profession, she does not try to explain it. Is there some institutional or commercial block to women's advancement? Or do those who avail themselves of *haute coiffure* simply prefer the ministrations of men? Cox never tells us what she thinks.

Whatever its hidden meanings, the history of hairdressing is intimately tied to the development of technology, and Cox is at once enlightening and droll as she relates the uncertain efforts of capillary science. Take the matter of hygiene. Before the twentieth century, those few British women who washed their hair did so rarely. Most salons had no access to hot water. In an attempt to make some money and, it would seem, make their work more pleasant, hairdressers began to experiment with something called "dry shampooing": that is, washing hair with gasoline [petrol]. Cox describes some of the foreseeable consequences, including the demise of the young French actress, Mlle. Pascoline, when several drops of a lotion of petrol that her hairdresser was applying fell onto the stove and set fire to her hair and clothes. Or another unfortunate incident at the fashionable *maison* of Emile et Cie. in London, where another customer reported that she "heard an explosive 'boom' and rushed in to find Mrs. Samuelson on fire due to a spontaneous combustion of vapour from the wash." (33–4)

To avoid roasting their customers, hairdressers began to experiment with another chemical, most notably carbon tetrachloride. This substance was non-flammable, but it had an effect similar to that of chloroform. Its use led to several fatalities, one in the hairdressing department in Harrod's in 1909. Happily, as the century proceeded, better plumbing and hot-water heaters made shampooing less of a life-threatening adventure and, hence, a more frequent practice.

Of course, for some customers, principally bald men, the shampoo question remained academic. They had other hair-care needs. Theories to explain baldness abounded early in the century: that hair loss resulted from brushing hair too briskly or for too long; that it came from "exposure to evening mists" or the "over-enthusiastic application of bear's grease which 'rotted the roots'; or, more flatteringly, that it was the consequence of hair's having been 'burnt out' through brainpower." (30) Theories to reverse the process followed. Experts proposed various remedies. One hairdresser practiced a primitive form of hair transplant, whose main effect was to cause "the inflammation of the scalp and suppuration at the point of contact of the hair with the skin." (32) Others were no more successful.

Sometimes the techniques that redefined the profession owed very little to science. This was certainly true of the eponymous wave that made the French coiffeur, Marcel Grateau, so famous and so rich. Marcel, who used hot tongs and his fingers to create his inimitable waves, came to London to give a demonstration in 1908. The *Hairdressers' Weekly Journal* called it "the most remarkable gathering the hairdressing trade has ever witnessed." (140) The "marcel" remained a staple of hairdressing method through the 1930s, and was still being taught to students into the 1960s.

In the permanent wave, introduced in 1907, hairdressers discovered the perfect marriage between technology and commerce. Cox writes that the early process stuck women "under an extremely weighty mechanical contraption for hours at a time, looking and probably feeling as if they were undergoing some particularly nasty form of futuristic torture." (146–7) At first, hair had to be heated to over 200 degrees Fahrenheit. This made burns a constant danger, not to speak of electric shocks or over-heated rods, which might leave the client with a head full of melted plastic. Women nonetheless paid substantial sums to give their hair soft, durable waves. "Perm" technology advanced steadily through the century: from mechanical to chemical, from hot to cold, from the salon to the "home" perm and back. The permanent wave has been both central to changes in fashion and highly profitable for manufacturers and *salonniers*.

The technology of hair coloring has had a similar impact on hairstyles and the coiffeur's bottom line. The century began with the widespread use of such vegetable dyes as henna, and the technology took a great leap forward with the invention in 1909 of L'Oréal, the product that inaugurated the era of dependable, durable, largely non-toxic hair coloring. Increasingly, whether on the part of widows disguising the effects of

advancing age or teenage punks offending social convention and irritating
their parents, hair coloring has become a key part of the "statement" of
hairstyles.

A particularly significant moment in the history of colored hair came
in the 1930s with the vogue for platinum blonde, worn most famously
by Jean Harlow. Observers have often seen the platinum blonde as a model
of retrograde femininity, more sex than substance, a step backward from
the more assertive, less coquettish figure of the flapper, the feminine ideal
of the preceding decade. Contemplating the figure of Harlow, Cox takes
the opportunity to probe the deeper meaning of hairstyles and arrives at
a number of provocative conclusions, linking the platinum blonde to the
racial "hysteria" of the period, to class and gender issues, to working-
class hairdos and male domination.

This is a laudable exercise. In fact, it's what we've been led to expect
all along, a reflection on signifiers and significations, a conversation
between hairstyles and the deeper waters of social reality. Cox raises
several interesting points, but she ultimately gives us a pretty stock version
of cultural analysis, constructed more of cliché than of penetrating
deconstruction. She writes for example, that blondeness, and especially
the "cheap" blonde associated with the "easy" working-class woman, is
certainly a keystone of patriarchy and perhaps a sort of conspiracy,
climaxing in the "launch of Barbie as a blonde . . . a contemporary icon
to reinforce this mythology [of the golden-haired princess]." (162) Jean
Harlow's death at the age of twenty-six, Cox says, "exemplified the
cautionary tale of patriarchy."

I have two reservations about this "reading" of the platinum blonde.
First, Cox presents no evidence to support it, aside from one source taken
from the book, *Harlow: An Intimate Biography*, who confessed that, "To
me a blonde means good times and better sex." (160) No doubt there is
something to be made of the celebrity of "Grace Kelly, Kim Novak, and
the giggling Marilyn Monroe,"(162) but it is not so obvious that it
requires neither argument nor evidence to discover. Second, I am not
convinced that women reliably do what "patriarchy" instructs and that
cultural phenomena can thereby be explained simply by pointing to the
logic and interests of male hegemony. Why should blondeness be more
useful to patriarchy than, say, brunetteness? Besides, "Snow White"
Barbie has black hair—a blow against racism and patriarchy?

In any case, hydrogen peroxide was hardly the final word in hairdressing technology and fashion. The fifties were an age of "technological
optimism," of "space-age" hair, of DIY (Do-it-yourself) hairdressing, and
of "subservient, domesticated, femininity." (183) The 1960s, of course,
wrote goodbye to all that and ushered in a period of "natural," "unisex"
hairstyles. In fact, the sixties were a mixed bag for coiffeurs. On the one
hand, the flourishing counter-culture featured hair that was un-gendered
and undone, the very antithesis of hair-as-conspicuous-consumption. But
the rebellious sixties were also the "swinging" sixties, and the hairdressing

profession struggled to keep up. Cox mentions one American wigmaker who "marketed a fake moustache and beard set for two hundred dollars to transform the executive man into an instant swinger." (194–5) And she describes a general tarting up of salons, which now offered services like astrological readings, hair personality analysis, tanning, facials, even "indoor putting greens"—in an attempt to make a trip to the "stylist" feel like a "happening" rather than a chore. (198)

Finally, Cox leads us to the millennium, through the inevitable era of postmodern hair: Glam Rock, Gothic, Cyberpunk, etc. She has a short but hilarious discussion of the "reviled Mullet . . . worn by musclebound beery types and faded footballers." (212) You know the cut: short on top, long in the back—like vintage Michael Bolton. (There are apparently people who dedicate their lives to tracking down this unfortunate style and putting the results on the web. Cox lists a couple of Mullet websites. Check them out. They're hysterical.)

In the 1980s, Big Hair remained *de rigueur* for working-class women (Cox presumes), who adopted the models they saw on *Dallas* and *Dynasty*. Career women dressed their hair "for success" in the "power bob" or the discreet perm. The exception to this class rule (the rule is also bound to region, although Cox doesn't say so—in Texas, for example, even tailored career women wear Big Hair) lay on the formidable head of Margaret Thatcher, whose "large, heavily set and sprayed style gave the illusion of a hard helmet." (230–1) For the nineties, Cox examines the fashion impact of "Zoo TV," filled with "mall chicks with mulleted partners," the type immortalized by Paula Jones. (238) She looks at skinheads, Black men with shaved heads, with their "prison conno-tations," and the Nero cut, "ubiquitously associated with lad culture in Britain." (253) She nods approvingly at the inverse model of "girl power," where short skirts, platform shoes, and girly pouts become "a strategy of resistance [to patriarchy] . . . a subversion of fashion, to manipulate rather than to be manipulated." (259)

In the end, the author draws an appealing and highly amusing picture of contemporary fashion and society. The book is strewn with the silly opinions of "experts" trying to explain hairstyles. But there is a similar danger in Cox's own glib assertions about the links between hair and history, and I'm afraid that she falls victim to it, especially in the last chapter. As Cox reaches for profundity and clever turns of phrase, her survey of contemporary styles increasingly reads like a Sunday-supplement piece, replete with hip language and *Cosmo*-like cultural analysis: to wit, her comment on Kevin Keegan's perm, the "style for the trendy, sensitive yet macho guy about the wine bar." (241)

Moreover, beside the often very funny and pointed bits of pop anthro-pology, the author also deploys the heavy "po-mo" language of academia. See, for example, her comment on "girl power," or on punk women's slutty style, where, she writes, "an area traditionally signifying women's subordination was reappropriated as subversion. . ." (217–18)

*Good Hair Days*, then, is a rambling, anecdotal, informative, entertaining stroll through the modern history of British hairdressing. True, it does not tell us all that we would like to know about hairstyles: why some catch on and some don't, why Sassoon is lionized and Raymond forgotten; why punk ignites spontaneously, while Clairol needs to pour millions into its success and Brylcreem sinks into oblivion despite the best efforts of Madison Avenue. But it gives us a lot to consider. The lesson, I think, is that fashion retains a powerful element of randomness, driven here and there by the search for distinction and commerce. The rest is just dandruff.

*Fashion Theory*, Volume 4, Issue 3, pp.369–370
Reprints available directly from the Publishers.
Photocopying permitted by licence only.
© 2000 Berg. Printed in the United Kingdom.

# Call for Papers

Alexandra Palmer and Hazel Clark are putting together a book of essays
tentatively entitled: *Re-used and Reinterpreted: Second-Hand Dress*. It
is intended to address current research that highlights historical and
contemporary issues related to the second-hand clothing trades, consumption and practice of wearing second-hand dress. Papers dealing with
merchants, consumers, trade patterns, issues of gender, race and class from
a multicultural perspective are encouraged.

This book is intended to be of value to undergraduate and graduate
level students in women's studies, gender studies, design and fashion
history, and cultural history.

Please send a 4–6 page abstract with bibliography, a CV that includes your name, present position, list of publications and currrent research interests for consideration in this project.

If you are familiar with the work of scholars who may be interested in contributing to this book please ask them to contact us.

Send submissions by 15 March 2001 to: Dr. Alexander Palmer, Nora E. Vaughan Fashion Costume Curator, Textile & Costume Section – NEAC, Royal Ontario Museum, 100 Queen's Park, Toronto, Ontario, Canada, M5S 2C6 (email: alexp@rom.on.ca) or Dr. Hazel Clark (email: sdhazel@polyu,edu.hk).

# Notes for Contributors

Articles should be approximately 25 pages in length and *must* include a three-sentence biography of the author(s). Interviews should not exceed 15 pages and do not require an author biography. Film, exhibition and book reviews are normally 500 to 1,000 words in length. The Publishers will require a disk as well as a hard copy of any contributions (please mark clearly on the disk what word-processing program has been used).

*Fashion Theory: The Journal of Dress, Body & Culture* will produce one issue a year devoted to a single topic. Persons wishing to organize a topical issue are invited to submit a proposal which contains a hundred-word description of the topic together with a list of potential contributors and paper subjects. Proposals are accepted only after review by the journal editor and in-house editorial staff at Berg Publishers.

## Manuscripts
Manuscripts should be submitted to: *Fashion Theory: The Journal of Dress, Body & Culture*. Manuscripts will be acknowledged by the editor and entered into the review process discussed below. Manuscripts without illustrations will not be returned unless the author provides a self-addressed stamped envelope. Submission of a manuscript to the journal will be taken to imply that it is not being considered elsewhere for publication, and that if accepted for publication, it will not be published elsewhere, in the same form, in any language, without the consent of the editor and publisher. It is a condition of acceptance by the editor of a manuscript for publication that the publishers automatically acquire the copyright of the published article throughout the world. *Fashion Theory: The Journal of Dress, Body & Culture* does not pay authors for their manuscripts nor does it provide retyping, drawing, or mounting of illustrations.

## Style
U.S. spelling and mechanicals are to be used. Authors are advised to consult *The Chicago Manual of Style (14th Edition)* as a guideline for style. *Webster's Dictionary* is our arbiter of spelling. We encourage the use of major subheadings and, where appropriate, second-level subheadings. Manuscripts submitted for consideration as an article must contain: a title page with the full title of the article, the author(s) name and address, and a three-sentence biography for each author. Do not place the author's name on any other page of the manuscript.

## Manuscript Preparation
Manuscripts must be typed double-spaced (including quotations, notes, and references cited), one side only, with at least one-inch margins on standard paper using a typeface no smaller than 12pts. The original manuscript and a copy of the text on disk *(please ensure it is clearly marked with the word-processing program that has been used) must* be submitted, along with black and white *original* photographs (to be returned). Authors should retain a copy for their records. Any necessary artwork *must* be submitted with the manuscript.

### Footnotes

Footnotes appear as 'Notes' at the end of articles. Authors are advised to include footnote material in the text whenever possible. Notes are to be numbered consecutively throughout the paper and are to be typed double-spaced at the end of the text. (Do not use any footnoting or end-noting programs which your software may offer as this text becomes irretrievably lost at the typesetting stage.)

### References

The list of references should be limited to, and inclusive of, those publications actually cited in the text. References are to be cited in the body of the text in parentheses with author's last name, the year of original publication, and page number—e.g., (Rouch 1958: 45). Titles and publication information appear as 'References' at the end of the article and should be listed alphabetically by author and chronologically for each author. Names of journals and publications should appear in full. Film and video information appears as 'Filmography'. References cited should be typed double-spaced on a separate page. *References not presented in the style required will be returned to the author for revision.*

### Tables

All tabular material should be part of a separately numbered series of 'Tables'. Each table must be typed on a separate sheet and identified by a short descriptive title. Footnotes for tables appear at the bottom of the table. Marginal notations on manuscripts should indicate approximately where tables are to appear.

### Figures

All illustrative material (drawings, maps, diagrams, and photographs) should be designated 'Figures'. They must be submitted in a form suitable for publication without redrawing. Drawings should be carefully done with black ink on either hard, white, smooth-surfaced board or good quality tracing paper. Ordinarily, computer-generated drawings are not of publishable quality. Photographs should be black and white glossy prints (the publishers will not accept color) and should be numbered on the back to key with captions. Whenever possible, photographs should be 8 x 10 inches. All figures should be numbered consecutively. All captions should be typed double-spaced on a separate page. Marginal notations on manuscripts should indicate approximately where figures are to appear. While the editors and publishers will use ordinary care in protecting all figures submitted, they cannot assume responsibility for their loss or damage. Authors are discouraged from submitting rare or non-replaceable materials. It is the author's responsibility to secure written copyright clearance on *all* photographs and drawings that are not in the public domain.

### Criteria for Evaluation

*Fashion Theory: The Journal of Dress, Body & Culture* is a refereed journal. Manuscripts will be accepted only after review by both the editors and anonymous reviewers deemed competent to make professional judgments concerning the quality of the manuscript. Upon request, authors will receive reviewers' evaluations.

### Reprints for Authors

Twenty-five reprints of authors' articles will be provided to the first named author free of charge. Additional reprints may be purchased upon request.

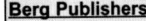

# Dress, Body, Culture
## from Berg Publishers

Series Editor: **Joanne B.Eicher**, University of Minnesota

Books in this provocative series seek to articulate the connections between culture and dress, which is defined here in its broadest possible sense as any modification or supplement to the body. Interdisciplinary in approach, the series highlights the dialogue between identity and dress, cosmetics, coiffure and body alterations and analyzes the meaning of dress in relation to popular culture and gender issues.

## 'Don We Now Our Gay Apparel'  NEW
### Gay Men's Dress in the Twentieth Century

**Shaun Cole**, The Victoria and Albert Museum, London

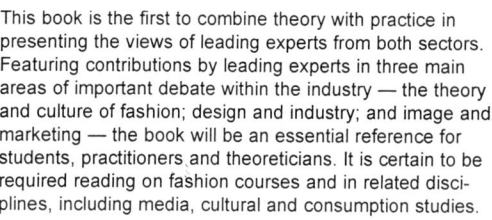

'Gay style actually sets trends. It's what straight people take fashion from.' *Tony Woodcock*

From the New Edwardians and muscle boys to Radical Drag and Genderfuck, gay men's dress has had a profound impact on fashion. However, it is easy to forget that, with few exceptions, gay men earlier in the century took great pains to conceal their sexual identity. Beginning with a look at the subcultural world of gay men in the early part of this century — particularly in New York and London — this fascinating book analyzes the trends in dress adopted by gay men as well as the  challenge gay style has made to mainstream men's fashion.

September 2000  224pp  illus, bibliog, index
Cloth       1 85973 415 4       £42.99     $65.00
Paper      1 85973 420 0       £14.99     $22.50

## Wearing Ideology  NEW
### State, Schooling and Self-Presentation in Japan

**Brian McVeigh**, Tôyô Gakuen University

Uniforms are not unique to Japan, but their popularity there suggests important linkages: material culture, politico-economic projects, bodily management, and the construction of subjectivity are all connected to the wearing of uniforms. This book examines what the donning of uniforms says about cultural psychology and the expression of economic nationalism in Japan. The author focuses particularly on student uniforms, but also examines 'office ladies' (secretaries), 'salary men' (white collar workers), service personnel, and housewives, who wear a type of uniformed dress.

September 2000  224pp  illus, bibliog, index
Cloth       1 85973 485 5       £42.99     $65.00
Paper      1 85973 490 1       £14.99     $19.50

## The Fashion Business  NEW
### Theory, Practice, Image

Edited by **Nicola White** and **Ian Griffiths**, both at Kingston University

This book is the first to combine theory with practice in presenting the views of leading experts from both sectors. Featuring contributions by leading experts in three main areas of important debate within the industry — the theory and culture of fashion; design and industry; and image and marketing — the book will be an essential reference for students, practitioners and theoreticians. It is certain to be required reading on fashion courses and in related disciplines, including media, cultural and consumption studies.

December 2000  256pp  illus, bibliog, index
Cloth       1 85973 354 9       £42.99     $65.00
Paper      1 85973 359 X       £14.99     $19.50

## The Culture of Sewing
### Gender, Consumption and Home Dressmaking

**Barbara Burman**, Winchester School of Art

Throughout its long history, home dressmaking has been a formative experience in the lives of millions of women. However, not only have the skills involved in home dressmaking been overlooked and marginalized, but the impact home dressmaking had on women's lives and broader socioeconomic structures also has been largely ignored. This book is the first serious account of the significance of home dressmaking as a form of European and American material culture.

November 1999  224pp  illus, bibliog, index
Cloth       1 85973 203 8       £42.00     $65.00
Paper      1 85973 208 9       £14.99     $19.50

**Berg Publishers**
**UK:** 150 Cowley Road, Oxford OX4 1JJ
**Order Hotline: (01202) 665 432 or fax (01202) 666 219**
**US:** c/o New York University Press
838 Broadway, Third Floor, New York NY 10003-4812
**Order hotline: 1 800 996 6987 or fax: (212) 995 3833**
*Website: http://www.berg.demon.co.uk*

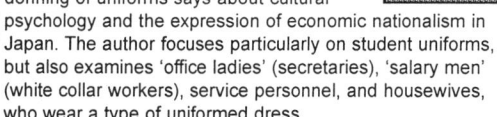

*Berg Publishers — The Dress Press*